Woodside Priory School

COMMUNITY COOKBOOK

THIRD EDITION

Woodside Priory School
302 Portola Road
Portola Valley, CA 94028-7897

Copyright © 2006 by Woodside Priory School, Portola Valley, CA

Published by Almaden Press, Santa Clara, CA

For information about purchasing this book contact the Woodside Priory School administrator at 650-851-8221

Manufactured in the United States of America

Woodside Priory School is an independent, Catholic, college preparatory school in the Benedictine tradition. Our mission is to assist students of promise in becoming lifelong learners who will productively serve a world in need of their gifts.

We believe in these Benedictine values:

Spirituality: God works in us, through us, and for us.

Hospitality: All are welcomed with honor and respect.

Integrity: Learning flourishes in an environment of honesty, trust, and personal responsibility.

Individuality: Every student has gifts to be discovered, nurtured, and treasured.

Community: Together we find strength and purpose in supporting one another.

We believe these values are made real in a community in which every student is known and loved.

The proceeds realized from the Woodside Priory Cookbook will be returned to the school.

ISBN-13: 978-0-9790849-0-4
ISBN-10: 0-9790849-0-3

Dedication

To the Tradition

of

Benedictine Education

and

to our Children

Table of Contents

Acknowledgements

Chairman	Virginia Taylor
Cookbook Committee	Linda Bader
	Marjorie Brent
	Dale Lachtman
	Margaret Herzen
	Mary Pham
	Felice Rebol (Koval)
	Laurie Schofield
Cover and Book Design	Linda Bader
Back Cover Pencil Drawing	Claire Watson 2009
Front Flap Text	Margaret Herzen
Back Flap Photograph	Father Martin Mager
Production	Felice Rebol (Koval)
Project Editor	Ryan Stern
Heritage Story and Recipe Writer	Margaret Herzen
Narrative History Writer	Laurie Schofield
Contributing Writers	Ryan Stern
	Virginia Taylor
Recipe Tester Coordinator	Dale Lachtman
Administrative Support	Tim Molak
	Josie Castaneda
	Pat Reed

The Cookbook Committee would like to give special thanks to Eric Stern and Steve Komorowski of Almaden Press, Santa Clara, CA for their kindness, patience and expertise in guiding us through self publishing this book.

Contributing Editors

Georgia Baba
Marjorie Brent
Cindy Davison
Ann Dingerson
Carol Fischer
Julie Helfrich
Tracy Kraczkowsky
Trixie Putnam
Mary Pham
Stellie Quinn
Virginia Taylor
Tamra Tehaney

Narrative History

Carolyn Dobervich
John Erkman
Igor Golden
Margaret Herzen
Father Martin Mager

Heritage Stories

Peter Agoston
Judith DeSzily
Carolyn Dobervich
Barbara Falk
Father Egon Javor
Father Maurus Nemeth
Mrs. Rosalia O'Grady
Mr. Ralph Oswald
Nathan Spears
Articles from the *Priory Parent*,
Priorities Magazine, the *Portola
Valley Almanac* and the *Palo Alto
Times*

Recipe Contributors

Bengta Baker Aboud	Mari-Lynn Earls	Susan Light	Stellie Quinn
Peggy Asprey	Lila Fitzgerald	Charlie Lombard	Felice Rebol
Linda Bader	Mark & Suzanne	Sue Lowe	Irina Sarkisov
Jane Bessin	Frappier	Martha Luemers	Laurie Schofield
Marjorie Brent	Linda Frasch	Cassie Maas	Marian Scheuer
Tim Conde	Karen Gregory	Pamela Martinson	Sofaer
Kimily Conkle	Betsy Haehl	Michelle Opperman	Virginia Taylor
Kevin Corkery	Roberta Harryman	Kelly Pettit	Sharon Traeger
Amanda Davison	Margaret Herzen	Mary Pham	Sylvia Trudelle
Wayne & Cindy	Paul Hickman	Lisa Plain	Patty Turnquist
Davison	Tracy Kraczkowsky	Francesca Purvin	Jean Young
Ann Dingerson	Ingrid Lai	Jeff Purvin	Sue Young
Liz Ditz	Roberta Landers	Trixie Putnam	Valerie Wookey

Recipe Testers

Susan Ahlstrom	Liz Ditz	Mary Pham
Georgia Babba	Mark & Suzanne Frappier	Francesca Purvin
Liz Bellock	Carol Fischer	Trixie Putnam
Christie Bilikam	Lila Fitzgerald	Stellie Quinn
Marjorie Brent	Emily Goldberg	Irina Sarkisov
Kevin Corkery	Margaret Herzen	Cindy Shove
Cindy Davison	Betsy Haehl	Virginia Taylor
Susan Dennis	Karen Hill	Tamra Tehaney
Ann Dingerson	Amy Magnuson	Sharon Traeger
Carolyn Dobervich	Kelly Pettit	Patty Turnquist
		Kathleen Dickey Varga

x

Introduction

Welcome to the 3rd edition of the Woodside Priory School Cookbook! As a person possessed with a deep love of cooking and finding much pleasure in the process of searching for and finding a perfect recipe, being asked to revive the tradition of the cookbook as a fund raising project, elated me. Here was our opportunity to share beloved recipes, which in themselves are a reflection of our community, a community that raises its children around the dinner table: learning manners, responsibility, respect, the art of conversation and, of course, the love of being together to enjoy the bounty of the table.

Proudly we launch this project to our perspective supporters. Along with our recipes, we want to give the reader a feel for our very special 50 year history. We are a community that celebrates a Benedictine education for our children. Here, we hope to share with you some of its unique aspects, told through a series of vignettes heading each chapter, weaving together the story of our family, where many of our teachers and staff live on campus, along side our monks and forty internationally diverse boarding students—a true family.

All of the funds raised from the sale of this special effort will go directly to helping create and support an education that nurtures not only the minds, but also the spirits of our children. We hope you enjoy our cookbook and may it bring you many years of happiness in your kitchen and at your family's table.

Virginia Taylor

᠀

Blue Cheese Bursts	4
Fois Gras Surprise Poppers	6
Artichoke Dip	8
Christmas Salsa	10
Festive Cheese Log	11
Mexican Party Dip	12
Warm Chili Sauce with Avocado	14
Mushroom Pâté	16
Spicy Crab and Ginger Salsa with Sesame Wontons	18
Crab Rangoon with Plum Sauce	20
Spinach & Cheese Phyllo Triangles	22
Stuffed Mushrooms with Spicy Sausage	24
Roasted Pepper and Artichoke Tapenade	26
Shanghai Spring Rolls with Sweet Chile Sauce	28
Wild Mushroom Tart	30
Baked Clams	32
Salmon Tartare	34

Appetizers

1

A European School in America

The story of Woodside Priory School begins a little more than 1,000 years ago with the founding of the Pannonhalma Abbey in Hungary. This Benedictine Abbey has been a major intellectual center throughout the centuries, not only as an important institution of learning for Benedictine monks, but also as a school for the most promising students in Hungary. Indeed, the library at Pannonhalma Abbey is renowned for its collection of over 300,000 works and for its ingenious medieval design. The clever placement of windows and mirrors allows sufficient natural lighting into the building to eliminate the need for artificial light during the day. This was an important factor in keeping the collection safe in the time when candles, and their smoke, could damage or destroy books and manuscripts.

After World War II, when Communism spread across Eastern and Central Europe, the monks at Pannonhalma realized that their freedom of thought and intellectual inquiry was in danger. Indeed, as Stalinism tightened its grip in Hungary, many monks, including Father Egon and his early colleagues at the Priory, fled Pannonhalma and came to America to continue their tradition of education and Ora et Labora, prayer and work.

They founded Woodside Priory School in 1957 with the blessing and financial help from many benefactors. The school was a European boarding school in America; the boys wore coats and ties, they studied Latin, German, and the classics, and classes were held six days a week. The students worked hard and discipline was strict. By the 1970's, however, the founding monks decided that Woodside Priory School needed a bit of Americanization To the students' relief, Saturday classes and coats and ties were dropped, and girls joined the student body in 1991, but one of the hallmarks of the European tradition remains today: soccer. In fact, when the Priory began, no other high school in the Bay Area had a soccer team, and the Priory boys played games against the local universities. To this day, the Woodside Priory soccer team is undefeated against Stanford University!

Blue Cheese Bursts

Lisa Plain discovered these delicious bursts consisting of sweet grape, strong blue cheese and nutty crunch of pistachio when they were served at a catered party. She asked for the ingredients and experimented until she was able to re-create this recipe for the bite-sized flavorful morsels. The round seedless red grape variety is easier to work with than the oval-shaped purple or green grape, and tends to have a crisper bite and sweeter flavor.

Lisa Plain
Alexandra 2008
Henry (Hap) 2006

Serves 6

6 ounces blue cheese, crumbled
4 ounces cream cheese, softened
20 red round seedless grapes
2/3 cup crushed pistachios

Blend blue cheese and cream cheese together until smooth. Refrigerate until well chilled. Wash, dry and chill grapes. It's very important to have grapes chilled and dry before proceeding. When the cheese is cold, take about two teaspoons cheese mixture (more or less depending on size of grapes) and flatten it slightly in your hand. Place a grape in the flattened cheese mixture and encase the grape in the cheese. Place the cheese-covered grapes on a cookie sheet covered with parchment or foil. Refrigerate until cold, approximately 45 minutes. Remove grapes from refrigerator and roll in crushed pistachio nuts to coat.

Tester's Comments: *Delicious! Frankly, the method for encasing the grapes in the soft cheese seems difficult at first, but after a short while you get the hang of it, and your productivity increases impressively! The trick to getting that nice layer of pistachio around the cheese covered grape is to roll the grapes over the chopped nuts, pressing a bit harder as you roll, so the grape picks up a generous layer of chunks of pistachio. The crunch imparted by the nuts, followed by the surprise grape beneath is what makes this recipe so awesome!*

Francesca Purvin

Fois Gras Surprise Poppers

Many of your guests will assume these familiar looking bite-sized, walnut covered treats are some sort of cheese hors d'oeuvre. Surprise!

Jeff Purvin
Colton 2011

Makes 30 Poppers

1 cup finely chopped walnuts
1½ cups (12 ounces) fois gras pâté, at room temperature
¾ cup balsamic vinegar
2 rounded teaspoons sugar
30 seedless red grapes, washed, dried and well chilled

Place the walnuts in a dish next to the fois gras. In a small skillet, place the vinegar and sugar and set aside.

In the palm of your hand form a small ball of pâté and flatten it slightly. Place the grape on the pâté and wrap the pâté around the grape to cover in about a ½ inch encasing. Roll the covered grapes into the chopped walnuts, pressing ever so lightly to get the walnuts to stick to the grape. Place on a cookie sheet and repeat until all grapes are done.

Heat the vinegar and sugar mixture over high heat until boiling. Boil for about 3 minutes, stirring constantly. Do not leave unattended. Remove from heat as soon as the sauce becomes syrupy. This will happen after it has been reduced by more than half.

Pour the sauce onto a flat, decorative serving dish so that a very thin layer of sauce fills the middle of the plate. This is an opportunity to create an interesting shape for presentation purposes, e.g. a large butterfly, square or triangle.

Lay the poppers on top of the sauce layer so that, when eaten, each popper has only a tiny amount of sauce on it. Refrigerate until ready to serve.

Note: Poppers should be thoroughly refrigerated before serving.

Artichoke Dip

We received two similar recipes for this popular appetizer. This one adds pimento but Trixie Putnam's had an additional ½ cup of Cheddar cheese, a few pickled jalapeños and was served with tortilla chips. Choose the one that sounds the best to you or create your own version.

Kelly Pettit
Angela 2008

Serves 6

1 cup mayonnaise

1 cup grated Parmesan cheese, divided

2 (14-ounce) cans artichoke hearts (not packed in oil), chopped

¼ cup (2 ounces) jarred pimento peppers, chopped

1¾ teaspoon garlic salt

1 teaspoon minced onion

1 teaspoon chives

Parmesan Pita Crisps (recipe follows)

Preheat oven to 350 degrees.

Blend together mayonnaise and ¾ cup Parmesan cheese. Add chopped artichoke hearts, pimentos, garlic salt and onion. Place in a shallow ovenproof serving dish and top with remaining Parmesan cheese. Bake for 30 minutes. Serve with Parmesan Pita Crisps.

Parmesan Pita Crisps

6 (6-inch) pita rounds
Olive oil
1¼ cup freshly grated Parmesan
Salt and pepper

Preheat oven to 325 degrees.

Divide each pita in half to create two thin rounds. On the smooth side, brush with olive oil, sprinkle with Parmesan cheese, and salt and pepper. Cut the round in half, then each half into three pieces, creating 12 triangular pita chips from the original piece. Arrange the triangles in a single layer on large baking sheets. Bake for approximately 12 minutes, until wedges are golden and just crisp. Cool completely. These can be stored up to 3 days, in an airtight container.

Christmas Salsa

Festive and easy, this salsa is surprisingly delicious. A woman in the aisle of Cost Plus World Market gave Cassie Maas this recipe when she saw her buying a salsa dish. Cassie went home, made it, and it was gone before anything else she served!

Cassie Maas
Kimberley Szabo 2009

Serves 6

2 jalapeños, seeded and chopped
1 tablespoon cilantro, coarsely chopped
½ red onion, peeled and quartered
½ teaspoon cumin
1 can red jellied cranberries

Place all the ingredients in a food processor and pulse until smooth. Serve with chips or crackers as an appetizer.

Tester's Comments: *This salsa is sweet and zesty. I would definitely make it again, and would consider putting it over cream cheese as an appetizer as well. The salsa received a thumbs up from my family!*

Carol Fischer and Betsy Haehl

Festive Cheese Log

While the colors of this appetizer make it perfect for a Christmas party, this quick-to-make dish can be adjusted for all occasions by substituting the red bell peppers with yellow or orange, or even roasting your own mix of all three.

Michelle Opperman
Christian 2009
Camilla 2012

Serves 6

1 log of goat cheese (11-ounce)
1 small (6-ounce) jar roasted red peppers, drained and cut into strips
10 fresh basil leaves, sliced into thin ribbons
½ cup pine nuts, lightly toasted in a 350-degree oven for 7 minutes

Being careful to maintain the log shape, unwrap goat cheese and place on a serving platter. Place red peppers on top of cheese. Sprinkle with basil and pine nuts. Serve with crackers or garlic crostini (sliced baguette brushed with garlic olive oil and broiled until golden).

Tester's Comments: *A nice delicate flavor and the beautiful combination of red and green on the white cheese make this recipe an excellent addition to an appetizer spread.*

Emily Goldberg

Mexican Party Dip

A staple recipe for Jeff Purvin when hosting a crowd, this dish is always a hit. Guests have been known to linger permanently beside this complex, multi-layered dip. Every bite is different and delicious!

Jeff Purvin
Colton 2011

Serves 12 as part of an appetizer buffet

4 medium, ripe (soft) avocados, mashed
1 large clove garlic, minced
2 tablespoons fresh lemon juice
½ teaspoon salt
¼ teaspoon pepper
¼ cup mild salsa
6 large sprigs of cilantro, stalks removed, leaves finely chopped
½ teaspoon cumin
1 cup sour cream
½ cup mayonnaise
1 package taco seasoning mix
2 (10½-ounce) cans Frito's bean dip, or use recipe below
1 cup chopped green onions, green parts only
3 medium tomatoes, seeded and chopped
1 cup seedless black olives, chopped
8-ounce package of shredded sharp Cheddar cheese
1 large bag of tortilla chips

Combine the avocados, garlic, lemon juice, salt, pepper, salsa, cilantro and cumin in a medium-sized bowl. Set aside.

In a separate bowl, combine the sour cream, mayonnaise and taco seasoning mix.

Spread the bean dip in a large, shallow glass or decorative serving dish (about 3 inches deep), completely covering the bottom of the dish. Carefully spread the avocado mixture on top of the bean dip, taking care to not disturb the bean layer. Spread the sour cream mixture on top of the avocado layer, taking care to not disturb the underlying layers. Sprinkle the onions, tomatoes, olives and cheese on top of the sour cream layer, completely covering the dip

Serve with a large bowl of tortilla chips.

Homemade Bean Dip

15-ounce can of pinto beans, drained
4 jalapeño slices, nacho style
1 tablespoon juice from bottled jalapeños
½ teaspoon salt
½ teaspoon sugar
½ teaspoon onion powder
¼ teaspoon paprika
⅛ teaspoon garlic powder
⅛ teaspoon cayenne pepper

Combine pinto beans with jalapeños, juice, salt, sugar, onion powder, paprika, garlic powder and cayenne in a food processor. Purée until smooth.

Warm Chili Sauce
with Avocado

When Betsy Haehl was growing up, her mother would serve this sauce inside one half of a warmed avocado – very rich, but a real treat for special occasions.

Betsy Haehl
Alicia Kriewall 2007

Serves 4

2 tablespoons sugar
2 tablespoons butter
4 tablespoons prepared chili sauce
3 tablespoons water
2 tablespoons vinegar
2 teaspoons Worcestershire sauce
5 bacon slices, cooked crisply and crumbled
2 avocados, split in half, seed removed and peeled
Salt

Heat sugar, butter, chili sauce, water, vinegar and Worcestershire in a double boiler. Add bacon at the last minute and mix well. Have ready a warmed avocado half, or cut avocado into quarters and slice thinly, leaving the narrow neck intact and fan out. Pour sauce over avocado. Salt to taste.

Tester's Comments: *We all loved it! I used Sriracha hot chili sauce (my favorite) and balsamic vinegar. The avocado's smoothness coupled with the zest and warmth of the sauce made this a real treat. This dish is heavy and rich, but it's also very flavorful and would make an excellent "stand alone" appetizer.*

Karen Hill

Mushroom Pâté

Discovered on the back of a mushroom brush package, this easy-to-make recipe needs to be made ahead of time, hence perfect for entertaining. You can really save time by using the pre-sliced mushrooms. It's a true crowd pleaser, even for people who are not fond of mushrooms.

Laurie Schofield
Jack 2003
Will 2006

Serves 8

1 pound mushrooms, cleaned and sliced
4 tablespoons (½ stick) butter
Salt to taste
1 tablespoon lemon juice
2 eggs, scrambled in butter
4 tablespoons finely grated Parmesan cheese
⅛ teaspoon cayenne pepper
½ teaspoon freshly ground pepper
⅓ cup chopped mixed fresh herbs (Italian parsley, chervil, tarragon or your favorite)
¼ teaspoon tarragon vinegar
8 tablespoons (1 stick) butter, softened
Melba toast or crackers

Melt 4 tablespoons of butter in a sauté pan. Add the mushrooms (salting well) and lemon juice; sauté for about five minutes, shaking the pan often until the mushrooms are cooked. Place the mushrooms and their liquid in a food processor and purée. Cool slightly. Add scrambled eggs and Parmesan cheese and pulse in to mix. Transfer to a bowl and stir in the cayenne and ground pepper, chopped herbs, vinegar and the softened butter. Season to taste with salt and more pepper if needed. Mix well and put in a crock and refrigerate overnight.

Serve with Melba toast or crackers.

~

Tester's Comments: *This will be a staple recipe in the Corkery household!*

Kevin Corkery

Spicy Crab and Ginger Salsa with Sesame Wontons

Served with crispy wonton chips, this Thai-inspired salsa provides a refreshing and unique twist on the "chips and salsa" concept. It's a great addition to any Asian fusion luncheon or appetizer spread. The Thai chili-garlic sauce can be found in the international foods section of most grocery stores, or at any specialty market. The wontons are fresh, and are found in the refrigerated section near the tofu.

Trixie Putnam

Matthew 2011

Kent graduated 8th grade in 1978

Serves 8

3 tablespoons rice wine vinegar
2 tablespoons vegetable oil
1 tablespoon lime juice
1 to 2 teaspoons Thai chili-garlic sauce or paste
1 teaspoon sesame oil
½ teaspoon salt
12 ounces lump crab meat, drained, picked over and shredded
1 cucumber, peeled, seeded and diced
2 green onions, sliced
2 tablespoons pickled ginger, chopped
Peanut oil
24 wontons
2 tablespoons sesame seeds, toasted
Salt

Whisk together rice wine vinegar, vegetable oil, lime juice, chili-garlic sauce, sesame oil and salt in a medium-sized bowl. Stir in crab meat, cucumber, onions and ginger. Cover and chill until ready to serve.

Pour peanut oil to a depth of ½ inch into a large skillet. Over medium heat, bring oil to approximately 300 degrees and fry wontons in batches, approximately 30 seconds on each side, or until golden. Drain on paper towels; sprinkle with sesame seeds and salt while hot.

Serve wontons with salsa.

Crab Rangoon
with Plum Sauce

We think this recipe, from CD Kitchen (cdkitchen.com), for crab Rangoon is the best we've tasted. The sweet and sour plum sauce perfectly matches the rich, creamy filling. These are surprisingly easy and quick to make, so double the recipe and freeze half. Cook them twice as long as the fresh version.

Trixie Putnam

Matthew 2011

Kent graduated 8th grade in 1978

Serves 12

½ pound crabmeat, picked over for shells
½ pound cream cheese, at room temperature
½ teaspoon A1 sauce
¼ teaspoon garlic powder
1 package wonton skins
2 egg yolks, mixed
Oil for frying
Plum Sauce (recipe follows)

Combine crab meat, cream cheese, A1 sauce and garlic powder, blending to a paste. Place one teaspoon of mixture on each wonton skin. Gather the 4 corners together (moisten fingers with egg yolk) and mash until it seals. Fill a deep saucepan ⅓ full of peanut, canola or vegetable oil. Heat oil to 350 degrees on a candy thermometer. Place three or four wontons at a time in the oil and deep fry until brown, about 30 seconds to one minute. Serve with Plum Sauce as soon as they come out of the oil.

Plum Sauce

1 cup plum preserves
½ cup water
2 tablespoons ketchup
2 tablespoons rice vinegar
2 teaspoons cornstarch mixed with 2 teaspoons water

In small saucepan over medium heat, combine plum preserves, water, ketchup and vinegar. Combine ingredients and bring to a boil in a small saucepan. Add cornstarch mixture until just thickened (you may not need all of it), stirring constantly. Serve hot or cold with Crab Rangoon.

Spinach & Cheese
Phyllo Triangles

This classic Greek appetizer is well worth the extra effort required by phyllo dough, which, despite being tricky at times, gets much easier to handle with practice. Once baked, the flaky delicate pastry triangle will melt in your mouth, revealing the lovely mix of melted feta cheese and spinach inside.

Trixie Putnam
Matthew 2011
Kent graduated 8th grade in 1978

Makes 33 pieces

1 egg
½ medium onion, chopped
4 ounces feta cheese, crumbled
4 ounces cream cheese
6 ounces frozen chopped spinach, thawed and drained well
1 teaspoon chopped parsley
1 teaspoon chopped fresh dill
½ teaspoon garlic powder
Salt and pepper to taste
1 package phyllo dough
1 stick butter, melted

Combine egg, onion and feta cheese in a food processor; pulse to mix. Add cream cheese; pulse two or three more times. Add spinach and seasonings; pulse just until mixture is blended. Transfer to a bowl and chill one hour.

Phyllo Dough

Preheat the oven to 400 degrees.

Note: Phyllo dough must be handled with care, since it is delicate, dries out quickly and will break. Proper defrosting is a must. Place frozen package in the refrigerator and let defrost for at least 4 hours or overnight.

Carefully unroll and unfold the phyllo package. Cover the entire package of phyllo with a slightly damp tea towel. Phyllo sheets are generally 16-by 22-inches. Take one sheet off the stack and brush the entire sheet liberally with melted butter. Top with another sheet. Cutting through both sheets, cut strips 2 inches wide by 16 inches long. Using one strip at a time, place a teaspoon of filling on one end of the strip. Fold one corner of the strip to the opposite side, forming a triangle and enclosing the filling. Continue folding (as you would an American flag) to the end of the strip, maintaining a triangular shape. Brush with melted butter and place on an ungreased cookie sheet. Repeat until filling is gone. Wrap up remaining phyllo sheets and store. Bake for about 20 minutes until lightly browned. Serve hot.

This recipe is perfect for freezing. Double or even triple the filling to make extras if you have the time. You can bake the frozen phyllo triangles without defrosting; simply increase the baking time by 5 minutes to 25 minutes.

Stuffed Mushrooms
with Spicy Sausage

Spicy sausage and the creamy, nutty richness of the Parmesan cheese makes these stuffed mushrooms a true burst of delicious flavor. This appetizer is great when throwing large parties, because it is quick to put together ahead of time and you can just pop the mushrooms in the oven before guests arrive. This recipe came from *Bon Appétit*.

Trixie Putnam
Matthew 2011
Kent graduated 8th grade in 1978

Makes 24

3 Italian hot sausages, casings removed
1½ teaspoons dried oregano
1 cup freshly grated Parmesan cheese (about 3 ounces), divided
½ teaspoon Worcestershire sauce
½ teaspoon garlic powder
8-ounce package cream cheese, room temperature
Salt and pepper
1 egg yolk
Olive oil
24 large (2-inch diameter) mushrooms, stemmed and wiped clean
⅓ cup dry white wine

Preheat oven to 350 degrees.

Heat large skillet over medium-high heat and add sausage, oregano and a bit of olive oil if needed. Cook sausage, breaking it into small pieces with the back of a fork or wooden spoon, until cooked through, about 7 minutes.

24

Using a slotted spoon, transfer sausage mixture to large bowl and cool. If mixture is in large pieces, you can pulse it in a food processor. Mix in ½ cup Parmesan cheese, Worcestershire sauce, and garlic powder, and then add in cream cheese. Season filling with salt and pepper; mix in egg yolk.

Brush a 15-by 10-by 2-inch glass baking dish with olive oil to coat. Brush cavity of each mushroom cap with white wine; fill with a scant tablespoon of filling and sprinkle with some of remaining Parmesan cheese. Arrange mushrooms, filling side up, in prepared dish. Prepare to this point, then cover and chill. Mushrooms can be made 1 day ahead. Bring to room temperature before baking.

Bake uncovered until mushrooms are tender and filling is brown on top, about 25 minutes.

Roasted Pepper and Artichoke Tapenade

Betsy Haehl served this tasty tapenade at a book club meeting and everyone wanted the recipe. It's fast, easy to prepare, and keeps well if made the day ahead, making it an ideal appetizer for dinner parties. Serve with Parmesan Pita Crisps (page 9).

Betsy Haehl
Alicia Kriewall 2007

Serves 8

1 (7-ounce) jar roasted red peppers, drained
1 (6-ounce) jar marinated artichoke hearts, drained (reserving marinade)
⅓ cup minced fresh parsley
¼ cup grated Parmesan cheese
¼ cup capers, drained
Olive oil (add enough to reserved marinade to equal ⅓ cup)
3 cloves garlic
1 tablespoon lemon juice
Salt and pepper
Parmesan Pita Chips (recipe follows)

Tapenade

Combine red peppers, artichoke hearts, parsley, cheese, capers, olive oil, garlic and lemon juice in food processor, pulsing until mixture is well blended and finely chopped. Season with salt and pepper and serve. (Can be made a day ahead of time.)

Tester's Comments: *This recipe was great! Next time I make it, I will try serving the tapenade over grilled vegetables and put it all over pasta. I used olive oil flavored Pam instead of olive oil for my second batch of pita crisps. I had three other people taste the crisps and no one could tell the difference between the sprayed pita and the brushed pita. It really saved a lot of time!*

Kelly Pettit

Shanghai Spring Rolls
with Sweet Chile Sauce

Fresh ginger, succulent pork and shrimp, and crunchy water chestnuts are wrapped up and fried into a tasty spring roll and topped off with a sweet-and-spicy chili sauce, great with any California fusion or Asian fusion menu. You'll want to purchase fresh wonton or egg roll wrappers, which can be found in the refrigerated section of your supermarket near the fresh pastas.

Trixie Putnam
Matthew 2006
Kent graduated 8th grade in 1978

Makes 15

2 eggs
½ pound fresh shrimp, peeled, deveined and finely chopped
½ pound ground pork
1 (8-ounce) can water chestnuts, drained and minced
1 (8-ounce) can bamboo shoots, drained and minced
3 cloves garlic, minced
2 green onions, diced
2 tablespoons minced fresh ginger
1 tablespoon soy sauce
⅛ teaspoon salt
⅛ teaspoon pepper
1 (12-ounce) package wonton or egg roll wrappers
Vegetable oil
Sweet Chile Sauce, recipe below
Lettuce leaves (optional)

Lightly beat one egg in a medium-sized bowl. Add shrimp, pork, water chestnuts, bamboo shoots, garlic, green onions, ginger, soy sauce, salt and pepper, mixing well. In a separate bowl, lightly beat remaining egg. Spoon

1 tablespoon of mixture into center of a wonton wrapper. Fold top right corner of the wrapper over filling, tucking tip of corner under filling, then fold top left and bottom right corners over filling. Lightly brush remaining corner with beaten egg. Tightly roll filled end toward bottom left corner, and gently press to seal. Continue with remaining wrappers.

Pour vegetable oil to a depth of 2 inches into a medium saucepan and heat to 350 degrees. Fry spring rolls, a few at a time, about 6 minutes or until golden. Drain on paper towels. Serve rolls with Sweet Chili Sauce and over lettuce leaves, if desired.

Sweet Chili Sauce

Makes 2 cups

1 (7-ounce) bottle hot chili sauce with garlic
½ cup water
½ cup rice wine vinegar
¼ cup sugar
¼ cup lemon juice
2 tablespoons chili paste

Stir together all ingredients until blended. Chill until ready to serve.

Tester's Comments: *This recipe can be tweaked a bit to taste. I eliminated the shrimp for one batch; Trixie recommended ground turkey for another batch. When filling the egg rolls, you may need to adjust the amount of filling depending on the type of wrapper. One tablespoon leaves the finished egg roll needing a bit more filling, while the 1 tablespoon in a wonton wrapper will spill a bit over the sides. If you are making this as an appetizer for a larger crowd, you can fry the rolls, and then reheat them in an oven before the party.*

Sharon Traeger

Wild Mushroom Tart

Sautéed wild mushrooms on their own are wonderful, but for culinary nirvana, add some crème fraîche and a crispy pie crust to create this delicious tart. This dish can be served as a first course with a spicy green salad or as a light luncheon meal. Open a bottle of a French burgundy to round out a complete vegetarian meal!

Mari-Lynne Earls
Jordon 2006

Serves 6 to 8

1 tablespoon unsalted butter
1 tablespoon olive oil
¾ pound mixed fresh wild mushrooms, sliced into bite-sized pieces
2 tablespoons shallots, finely chopped
1 teaspoon fresh thyme, finely chopped
Salt and pepper to taste
½ cup crème fraîche
½ cup heavy cream
1 whole egg
1 large egg yolk
1 pie crust

Preheat oven to 350 degrees.

Place pie crust in freezer for at least 30 minutes; line with foil and fill with pie weights, beans or rice. Place in oven and bake for 20 minutes. Remove foil and weights and cook for an additional 5 minutes. Set aside to cool. Reduce heat to 325 degrees.

Melt butter with oil in large sauté pan over medium-high heat. Add mushrooms, shallots and thyme; season with salt and sear, undisturbed, until mushrooms are browned on one side. Stir and continue to cook until mushrooms are tender and liquid has evaporated. Season again with salt if needed, and then pepper to taste. Mixture should be dry. Cool.

Whisk together crème fraîche, heavy cream, egg and egg yolk. Place mushrooms evenly over the bottom of the pie crust; pour cream mixture over mushrooms.

Bake at 325 degrees for 30 minutes or until set. Cool.

Tester's Comments: *Using frozen pie dough did not detract from this fabulous dish. I brushed the bottom of the dough with egg wash (one egg white mixed with a teaspoon of water) after I removed the foil. Five more minutes in the oven was enough to set the egg to help seal in the crispy texture.*

Mary Pham

Baked Clams

The key to this wonderful, flavorful clam dish is to use homemade breadcrumbs. They are easy to make, and well worth the effort. This dish can be served as an appetizer, placing all the clams on a platter and offering small forks for easy eating. Or, you can serve them as a first course, placing four or five shells on each plate.

Suzanne and Mark Frappier
Allie 2011

Serves 4

12 clams
1 cup homemade, plain breadcrumbs (recipe follows)
¼ cup chopped fresh parsley leaves
1 tablespoon finely chopped garlic
½ cup olive oil
Salt to taste

Preheat the oven to 350 degrees.

Clean and shuck the clams, making sure to remove all sand and grit from the clams and their shells.

Chop the clams then lightly salt and distribute them among the shells. You should have enough meat to distribute into about 16 shells. Arrange the shells with clams on a baking sheet.

In a small bowl, toss together the bread crumbs, parsley, and garlic. Stir the olive oil into the breadcrumb mixture. It should be moist but not oily. Salt to taste.

Fill each shell with a portion of the topping mixture, spreading it evenly over the clams to the edge of the shell. The topping should be at least ⅛-inch thick.

Bake for approximately 5 minutes until the topping begins to brown slightly. Remove from the oven and increase oven temperature to broil. Place the clams under broiler and cook until golden brown, about 1 minute. Serve immediately.

Homemade Breadcrumbs

Take a loaf of day old bread, cube it and place into a food processor. Pulse until the bread starts to break down, and then process until it turns into crumbs. If the bread is not dry enough, place it onto a baking sheet and dry in a 300 degree oven for 5 to 10 minutes, depending on how stale your bread is. Do not let the bread brown.

Salmon Tartare

The brilliant pink salmon is stunning mixed with the green parsley and capers, yellow lemon zest and white shallots. This is a wonderful variation on your typical Ahi tuna tartare. The marinated cucumber ribbons are not necessary but add a nice tart crunch to the smooth salmon.

Suzanne and Mark Frappier
Allie 2011

Serves 8

12 ounces fresh salmon, skin, gray flesh and pin bones removed
2 tablespoons chopped shallots
1½ teaspoons lemon zest (grated, peel only)
1½ tablespoons fresh lemon juice
3 tablespoons finely chopped parsley
1 tablespoon olive oil
1 teaspoon capers, plus a dash of the juice
¼ teaspoon Tabasco sauce
Salt and pepper to taste
Cucumber ribbons (recipe follows)

Cut salmon into small cubes, approximately ¼-inch square. In a bowl, mix together salmon, shallot, lemon zest, lemon juice, parsley, olive oil, capers, caper juice and Tabasco. Season to taste with salt and pepper. Refrigerate at least 1 hour and up to 24 hours.

Serve with crackers or pumpernickel bread with the cucumber ribbons placed on a platter for guests to help themselves. Or, make up the individual

34

canapés by placing a few teaspoons of tartare on the bread and decoratively fold the ribbon on top.

Cucumber Ribbons

1 English cucumber, peeled
¼ teaspoon salt
¼ teaspoon sugar
¼ teaspoon ground pepper
2 teaspoon rice wine vinegar, plain or seasoned
Capers and chopped chives to garnish

Use a vegetable peeler to shave strips lengthwise from an English cucumber. Stop shaving once you have hit the seeds. Cut in 4-inch long ribbons. You should have about 2 cups. Place in a bowl and toss with the salt, sugar, pepper and rice wine vinegar. Garnish with capers and chives.

Soups

A Benedictine Education

Benedict of Nursia founded the Benedictine Order in 529 in Italy. His emphasis on work and prayer signified a dramatic change in the way monasteries related to the outside world. Benedictine monks showed in their daily work that physical labor and learning have the same inherent dignity as religious devotion. No longer did monks have to wander the land to ask for food and money from benefactors, since each monastery included all the facilities that were necessary for self-sufficiency. By the ninth century, the Rule of Saint Benedict had permeated monasteries across Europe. Monastic communities became important centers of learning not only as repositories of knowledge in the form of libraries and scriptoria, but also as centers of teaching.

The Rule of Saint Benedict emphasizes learning, balance, respect and community, and is a remarkably fitting model for a school in the 21st century. Benedictine education easily embraces people of diverse cultures, races and religions because each person is honored and respected not only as an individual, but also as a member of the community. Priory students and faculty quickly learn that the Benedictine values of spirituality, hospitality, integrity, individuality and community inform all the interactions between the members of our community. We strive to live each day with a sense of awareness of the importance of what we are engaged in, and we know that our lives will be enriched when we use our personal gifts to do good works for others. Saint Benedict begins his Rule urging the reader to "listen with the ear of your heart," and ends by encouraging the reader that, after living with Benedictine values, "you can set out for the loftier summits…of teaching." Priory students go out into the world well prepared for the challenges of the "loftier summits" of college and adult life, ready to use their talents to accomplish great things.

Gazpacho

Patty Turnquist was given this recipe 20 years ago from a dear friend, and it is still as fresh and as usable today as it was when she received it. It is a tried-and-true combination of garden fresh tomatoes, onions, cucumbers and peppers, simply added to tomato juice seasoned with lemon. Perfectly ripe ingredients and simplicity are the keys in this soup. Truly wonderful on a hot summer night.

Patty Turnquist
Eric 2012

Serves 6

1 garlic clove
6 large tomatoes, peeled, seeded and chopped to your liking
2 cucumbers, peeled, seeded and chopped to your liking
½ cup chopped green or red bell pepper, or a combination of both
½ cup chopped yellow or white onion
2 cups tomato juice
⅓ cup olive oil
3 tablespoons lemon juice
Salt and pepper to taste
Dash of Tabasco

Garnish

Chopped parsley
Croutons

Cut the garlic in half and rub a large (10 cup) glass bowl with the cut side. Add the tomatoes, cucumbers, peppers, onion, tomato juice, olive oil and lemon juice. Stir until combined. Season to taste with salt, pepper and Tabasco.

If desired, serve with chopped parsley and croutons.

Cream of Asparagus Soup
with Crab

The addition of sweet crab adds elegance to this light, beautifully colored soup. If you have time pick a freshly cooked crab, but prepared crab meat works just fine. The chlorophyll in parsley brightens the color of the soup but the flavor is not changed if you omit this step. The recipe is adapted from George Pierre of the Le Bec Fin Restaurant in Philadelphia. His cookbook is one of Virginia Taylor's favorites for French cooking with flair.

Virginia Taylor
Geoff 2006
Anna 2007
Katie 2011

Serves 8

4 pounds asparagus, tough ends removed, tips saved and stems cut in 1-inch lengths
4 tablespoons unsalted butter
2 medium onions, chopped
2 ribs celery, sliced
2 garlic cloves, minced
4 cups chicken stock, canned is fine
1 cup heavy cream
Salt and white pepper to taste

Garnish

1 bunch Italian parsley, stems removed (optional)
½ pound jumbo lump crab meat, picked clean
Reserved asparagus tips

42

In a medium stockpot, melt the butter over medium heat and lightly sauté the onions, celery and garlic until translucent, about 5 min. Add asparagus stalks and chicken stock; bring to a boil, lower the heat and cook, covered at a low simmer for 15 minutes or until asparagus stocks are just tender. Overcooking will render the asparagus tasteless; undercooking will create a chunky purée.

Strain the vegetables from the stock and purée them, in a blender or food processor with just enough liquid to fully purée the asparagus. Add the remaining stock to the purée and, to create a fine, French silky soup, strain the soup through a fine mesh strainer or food mill attached with the finest disc. Push hard on the vegetable solids to extract all the flavor from the pulp. While this step is not necessary, it creates a wonderful mouth feel to the soup. Stir in cream and season to taste with salt and pepper.

Prepare the garnish while the asparagus is cooking. Create an ice bath by placing ice in a medium-sized bowl and fill with cold water. Bring a small saucepan of water to a boil and season to taste with salt, add the reserved asparagus tips and cook until they turn bright green and are tender crisp, about 1 to 2 minutes. Remove tips, reserving the cooking water, and place in the ice bath. Once cooled, drain and dry asparagus well. Add the parsley to the cooking liquid and return to a boil. Lower heat and simmer, uncovered, for 5 minutes. Drain the leaves and refresh the parsley under cold water to set the color. Pulse the leaves in a blender or food processor with just enough cold water to create a smooth purée. Add enough to the soup to create a bright green color. This does not add flavor to the finished product, just enhances the color, so it is an optional, very French step.

Bring the soup back to a boil and then simmer. Remove one cup of soup and place in a small saucepan. Add crab meat, asparagus tips and season with salt and pepper. Heat for one minute. Ladle the remaining soup into hot soup bowls, then divide the crabmeat and asparagus mixture evenly among the portions, creating a mound in the middle of the bowl. This works best in shallow soup bowls. Serve immediately.

Green Corn Soup

Laurie Schofield's mother learned this recipe from a woman who spent years studying and teaching Mexican cuisine. Pair this flavorful soup with quesadillas for a Mexican version of a soup and sandwich meal.

Laurie Schofield
Jack 2003
Will 2006

Serves 6

½ onion, chopped
4 tablespoons butter
1 clove garlic, chopped
⅔ cup salsa verde (Herdez brand)
5 cups chicken stock (approximately)
1½ pounds frozen corn, slightly thawed (or 4½ cups fresh kernels)
½ pound frozen peas, slightly thawed
3 large lettuce leaves (iceberg, romaine, or your choice)

Sauté onion and garlic in butter until onion is soft. Add salsa verde and cook for an additional minute; set aside. Purée the corn, peas and lettuce leaves in a food processor, adding about 1 cup of stock to thin the mixture. Add the purée to the onion mixture and slowly stir in the remaining broth to your desired thickness. Heat and simmer about 20 minutes, covered, until the soup thickens slightly and loses its electric green color.

Tomato Basil Soup

Here's an excellent way to enjoy tomato basil soup all year long. This recipe using good quality canned tomatoes is easy to prepare and low in fat and calories. For a more filling, but still light meal, serve with a side of foccacia bread topped with melted or fresh mozzarella cheese.

Betsy Haehl
Alicia Kriewall 2007

Serves 6

2 teaspoons olive oil
3 garlic cloves, minced
3 cups fat-free, low-sodium chicken broth
¾ teaspoon salt
3 (14.5 ounce cans) Muir Glen fire roasted diced tomatoes, with their
   juice

2 cups lightly packed fresh basil leaves, thinly sliced
Basil leaves for garnish (optional)

Heat oil in a large saucepan over medium heat. Add garlic; cook 3 seconds, stirring constantly. Stir in the broth, salt and tomatoes; bring to a boil. Reduce heat; simmer 20 minutes. Stir in basil.

Using either a hand blender, food processor or regular blender, emulsify half the soup, processing until smooth. Pour puréed soup back into the saucepan and repeat procedure with remaining soup. Reheat. Garnish with basil leaves, if desired.

Curried Apple and Butternut Squash Soup

With its unique contrast between the earthy squash and the crisp apple, this is a hearty and flavorful soup. Although there are many types of curry available, we prefer to use sweet yellow curry, which usually appeals to a wide range of tastes.

Betsy Haehl
Alicia Kriewall 2007

Serves 6

2 cups chopped sweet onions
6 cups (about 3 pounds) cubed and peeled butternut squash
2 medium Granny Smith apples, cored, peeled and chopped
2 tablespoons olive oil
½ teaspoon salt
1½ teaspoons to 1 tablespoon curry powder, depending on taste
3½ cups (or more as needed) low-sodium chicken broth

Preheat oven to 400 degrees.

Place onions, butternut squash and apples on a jelly roll pan and drizzle with oil and salt; toss to coat. Roast in preheated oven for 35 minutes until brown spots appear.

Place vegetables and curry powder in a stockpot and cover with the chicken broth. Bring to a boil then reduce the heat and cook, covered, for 15 minutes.

Purée soup in batches in a blender or food processor (covered with a towel to avoid the hot soup exploding from the blender) or emulsify with a hand blender. Return soup to the pot and season with salt and pepper. Add more broth if too thick. Serve hot. Can be made one day in advance, and then warmed before serving.

⤳

Tester's Comments: *The complex flavors are delicious! A dollop of crème fraîche is a nice garnish on the colorful soup. I roasted the vegetables and fruits in my convection oven (spread evenly over one large baking sheet), which significantly decreased the overall cooking time to about 15 to 20 minutes.*

Emily Goldberg

Dal Soup

This lentil soup has a lovely, light flavor without being too rich. Massur dal and garam masala are available at Indian supermarkets and sometimes in the international section of a quality market. This is excellent served with a side of naan, (Indian flatbread).

Marjorie Brent
Laura 2004
Ian 2007

Serves 8

2 cups split massur dal (red lentils)
4 cups water
2 teaspoons salt
2 tablespoons butter
2 large onions, finely sliced
1 teaspoon peeled and grated ginger root
2 large cloves garlic, pressed
2 serrano chilis split in half lengthwise
1 teaspoon garam masala
2 cups whole milk
¼ cup red wine vinegar
½ teaspoon salt

In a 3-quart saucepan, bring massur dal, water and 2 teaspoons salt to a boil over moderate heat. Lower the heat and simmer, uncovered, for 5 minutes, then simmer partially covered, stirring frequently, until the dal is soft, about 15 minutes. Remove from heat, mash with the back of spoon and set aside.

Heat butter in a 5-quart pot over moderate heat. Add onions and sauté, stirring often, until transparent and limp. Add the ginger, garlic and chilies and continue to sauté, stirring often until the onions are golden. Add the garam masala and cook, stirring for 1 minute. Add the mashed dal, mix thoroughly, then add the milk and mix well. Bring to a boil over a low flame. Add the vinegar, and ½ teaspoon salt; stir and cook 1 more minute. Remove from the heat, pick out and discard the chili pieces (4 in total). Serve immediately.

Tester's Comments: *This dish has a nice, spicy/nutty flavor that still tastes healthy. I started cooking the onion mixture while the massur dal was cooking to shorten the overall preparation time. I will definitely make it again!*

Kevin Corkery

Minestrone

The use of black beans, rather than the staple garbanzo, renders this variation of the traditional "no meat" minestrone unique. Adapted from the *New Basics Cookbook*, it is perfect for that light but satisfying winter meal. Double the recipe and freeze half for a quick meal on a busy day.

Marjorie Brent
Laura 2004
Ian 2007

Serves 8

3 tablespoons unsalted butter
4 cloves garlic, minced
2 medium carrots, diced
1 large onion, diced
2 medium leeks (white part only), diced
4 cups chicken stock (canned is fine)
2 cups beef stock (canned is fine)
3 cups cabbage, finely sliced
2 medium zucchini, sliced ½-inch thick
1 small potato, peeled and diced
6 ounces tomato paste
2 teaspoons dried oregano
2 teaspoons dried basil
1 teaspoon pepper
Salt
1 (16 ounce can) black beans, rinsed and drained
4 medium plum tomatoes, peeled, seeded and diced
½ cup elbow macaroni
Grated Parmesan cheese

Melt butter in a large soup pot. Add garlic, carrots, onion and leeks. Cook covered, over medium heat, until vegetables are wilted, approximately 10 minutes, stirring occasionally.

Add chicken and beef stocks, cabbage, zucchini, potato and tomato paste. Stir to combine, bring to a boil and reduce heat. Add oregano, basil, salt (to taste) and pepper. Simmer, covered, over low heat for 15 minutes.

Add beans, tomatoes and pasta. Simmer until pasta is done, approximately 10 minutes. Adjust seasonings and serve with Parmesan cheese.

Tester's Comments: *Our family likes a little meat for dinner. So before I melted the butter to cook the vegetables, I sautéed a pound of spicy turkey sausage (casings removed) in the stockpot until cooked, then removed it to a separate bowl before continuing with the vegetables. I also added a pinch of red pepper flakes to the vegetables for added spice. I added the cooked sausage in with the beans, tomatoes and pasta and finished the recipe as indicated. It received a huge thumbs up from my family.*

Betsy Haehl

Roasted Red Pepper Soup

Rancho La Puerta is not only a fantastic place to spend a week but has also provided us with this colorful soup. The original recipe called for red and green peppers but Felice felt the green peppers imparted a bitter flavor so she modified it by using only red. No need to be precise when chopping the vegetables, it is a puréed soup and your nice chopping will not be noticed in the blender. This soup is easy once the peppers are roasted.

Felice Rebol
Jake 2012

Serves 6

½ teaspoon olive oil
½ medium onion, coarsely chopped
½ carrot, coarsely chopped
1 celery rib, coarsely chopped
4 garlic cloves, chopped
½ medium baking potato, peeled and cut into chunks (½ inch or so)
6 roasted red bell peppers, coarsely chopped (recipe follows)
4 cups basic vegetable stock (homemade or canned stock)
1 teaspoon chopped fresh oregano
½ teaspoon chopped fresh thyme
Salt and freshly ground black pepper to taste
Thyme sprigs for garnish (optional)

Heat the oil over medium heat in a large saucepan. Sauté onions, carrots and celery for 5 to 6 minutes, until onion is golden. Add garlic, potato and roasted peppers and cook an additional 5 minutes, stirring periodically. Add the stock and simmer, covered, for 15 minutes or until potato is tender.

Let soup cool a bit, then add the oregano and thyme. Purée in a food processor or blender for about 10 to 20 seconds depending on desired consistency. Return to the pot and bring to a simmer. Season to taste with salt and pepper. Serve garnished with thyme sprigs if desired.

Roasted Peppers

You can broil, grill or roast your peppers directly on the flame of your gas burner. The object is to blacken the skin then steam the peppers in a plastic bag to aid in peeling.

Broiler Method: Prep your peppers by cutting the top and bottom off the peppers to expose the seeds. Halve the peppers and remove the seeds and the white vein. Press the pepper flat, skin side up, and place on a cookie sheet. Broil about 3 inches from your heat source until the skin is blackened. Place in a plastic bag until cool. Peel.

Grill or Gas Burner Method: Place the whole pepper on the grill or burner and let sit until black, about 2 to 3 minutes. Continue by rotating the pepper until the entire skin is blackened. Place in a plastic bag until cool.

When peppers are cool enough to handle, hold stem and pull out core to gently remove the roasted skin and seeds. Do not wash the peppers or you will wash away the flavor.

Golden Pepper Bisque

Now that you have perfected your technique for roasting peppers from the previous Roasted Red Pepper Soup, try this version using yellow peppers. The ingredients are similar but the proportions are different—a true lesson on how forgiving soups can be.

Amanda Davison 2000
Wayne and Cindy Davison, parents

Serves 6

1 tablespoon olive oil
1 large onion, chopped
2 large yellow bell peppers (about 1 pound), roasted and peeled (see Roasted Red Pepper Soup; page 52).
1 pound thin-skinned potatoes, peeled and cut into ½-inch chunks
¾ pound carrots, cut into ½-inch chunks
1 large stalk celery, thinly sliced
6 cups low-sodium chicken or vegetable broth
Extra-virgin olive oil
Salt and pepper
Shredded dry Ricotta or Parmesan Cheese
Garlic Croutons, recipe included

In a 5- to 6-quart saucepan, combine olive oil and onion; cook over medium-high heat, stirring occasionally, until onion is lightly browned, about 10 minutes. Add roasted bell peppers, potatoes, carrots, celery and broth. Bring to a boil; then reduce heat, cover and simmer until carrots are soft to bite, about 20 to 25 minutes. Let cool.

Strain the vegetables from broth, saving broth. Place vegetables in a blender or food processor and process with a cup of broth until smooth. You may

54

need to do this in batches. Transfer purée back into saucepan, adding broth to yield the right consistency. Season to taste with salt and pepper. Reheat soup and ladle into wide bowls. Garnish with flavorful olive oil, cheese and croutons.

Garlic Croutons

1 tablespoon olive oil
1 clove garlic, minced or pressed
3 slices French or sourdough sandwich bread, cut into cubes
Salt and pepper to taste

In a small bowl, combine oil, garlic and 1 tablespoon water. Spread bread cubes on a nonstick 10- by 15-inch baking sheet; brush evenly with oil mixture. Season to taste with salt and pepper. Bake in a 350-degree oven until croutons are crisp and golden, about 10 to 12 minutes.

If made ahead, let cool completely on a baking sheet on a rack; store in an airtight for up to 2 days.

Tortilla Soup

What makes this 15-minute soup so special is the condiments that are served with the broth. Be adventurous and use this recipe as your platform. Consider adding freshly cut corn, black beans, cubed zucchini or sliced Serrano chiles. While we recommended frying your own tortilla strips, to save time, crumble in good quality, store bought tortilla chips instead.

Virginia Taylor
Geoff 2006
Anna 2007
Katie 2011

Serves 8

¼ cup vegetable or peanut oil
1 white onion, chopped
1 clove garlic, minced
1 teaspoon Chipotle chili powder, or to taste
2 cups chopped tomatoes, peeled and seeded, fresh or canned
8 cups chicken broth, divided, canned is fine
3 cups shredded cooked chicken

Condiments

Fried tortilla strips
Crumbled Queso Ranchero
Grated Jack and Cheddar cheese
Avocado cubes
Shredded iceberg lettuce or cabbage

Chopped cilantro
Lime wedges

56

Warm the oil in a saucepan over medium heat; add onion and garlic and sauté for 3 minutes. Add Chipotle chili powder and continue to cook until onion is translucent, about 3 more minutes. Add tomatoes and cook for two minutes. Add 1 cup of the broth and bring to a boil. Turn heat off and let cool. Blend the soup base until well pureed. Place back into the saucepan and add remaining broth. Add chicken and reheat.

For serving, place condiments in decorative bowls. Let each individual place their chosen toppings into their bowl. Ladle hot soup over condiments and enjoy.

Chicken and Wild Rice Soup

This great supper soup comes from *Cooking Light* magazine. It is rich in flavor and texture, but is relatively low calorie. Quick-cooking wild rice may be difficult to find, but is usually available at specialty markets such as Whole Foods. The recipe also works with standard wild rice, it will just take longer to cook.

Irina Sarkisov
Katya 2006

Serves 8

2 cups cooked wild rice (1 cup raw)
Cooking spray
1 cup chopped onion
2 garlic cloves, minced
3 cups fat-free, low-sodium chicken broth
1½ cups peeled, cubed potato
3 cups 2 percent, or reduced-fat milk
⅓ cup all-purpose flour
10 ounces light processed cheese, cubed (such as Velveeta Light)
2 cups chopped roasted chicken breasts (about 2 breasts)
½ teaspoon freshly ground black pepper
¼ teaspoon salt
¼ cup chopped fresh parsley (optional)

Heat a large Dutch oven over medium heat and coat with cooking spray. Add onion and garlic and sauté 3 minutes. Add broth and potato and bring to a boil over medium-high heat. Cover, reduce heat, and simmer 5 minutes or until potato is tender.

Combine milk and flour, stirring well with a whisk. Add the milk mixture to potato mixture whisking constantly. Cook 5 minutes or until slightly thickened, stirring frequently. Remove from heat. Add cheese, stirring until cheese melts. Stir in rice, chicken, pepper and salt. Garnish with parsley, if desired.

Tester's Comments: *The prep time for this recipe is about 45 minutes, but it can be prepared even faster if you pre-cook the chicken and rice, and have them ready to add when you begin the soup. For some variety, you might want to add a bit of fresh lemon juice, curry, fresh herbs or flavors of your liking.*

Cindy Davison

60

Salads

The Founders

The seven young priests and monks who founded Woodside Priory School were Fathers Emidius, Christopher, Benignus, Egon, Leopold, Stanley and Achilles. They were all experienced high school and college teachers, with a plethora of advanced degrees from American and European universities. Arriving on the bare hill in Portola Valley, they undertook countless hours of both physical labor and planning to ensure that Woodside Priory School would have the physical and intellectual environment most conducive for a first-class college preparatory education.

Father Egon, in his role as Prior, not only located the land in Portola Valley upon which to build the new school, but also found and nurtured a community of benefactors in the San Francisco Peninsula area who shared the monks' vision of a Benedictine school for boys. In addition to the never-ending task of ensuring the financial well-being of the school, Father Egon taught the required senior Western Civilization class. His students remember this course as a "marvelous survey that was filled with humor, wisdom and insights into many of the difficult events in history." Many recall this rigorous class as the perfect foundation for college academics.

Father Christopher was headmaster and taught senior philosophy. Students were challenged by his curriculum that spanned the centuries from Plato and Aristotle to Kant and Hegel. A former student describes Father Christopher as a demanding and wise teacher who inspired both with encouragement and high expectations. "Every so often there would be a paper that had really missed the point. Father Christopher would hold up the paper between two fingers as if it were a dead animal and solemnly—but with good humor— refer to it as a 'miserable failure!'" Father Christopher was also a sports enthusiast who made sure that the new school had a proper soccer field. He could often be seen walking up and down the field picking up rocks and putting them in the bucket he carried along.

To the founding monks we owe deepest gratitude and respect. The Woodside Priory School of the 21st century seems on the surface so different from that of fifty years ago. Yet the school community of which we are such fond members has been built, literally and figuratively, on the vision and labor of those first men who arrived in Portola Valley in 1956.

Aegean Salad

This salad pairs wonderfully with any of your Mediterranean menus, but it's a must with the Rack of Lamb with Mint Vinaigrette (page 224) and Cabbage Rice (page 251). The olives flavor the dressing and the dressing flavors the olives. The key to developing that flavor is to let the dressing rest with the olives for a full 30 minutes. For an even more Mediterranean feel, throw in a few capers along with the feta cheese.

Stellie Quinn
Cory 2011

Serves 6

Oregano Dressing

1 tablespoon red wine vinegar
2 teaspoons lemon juice
1 clove garlic, minced or pressed
½ teaspoon salt
½ teaspoon dried oregano
⅛ teaspoon coarsely ground pepper
¼ cup olive oil
½ cup pitted moist Greek olives, cut in half

Salad

4 cups red leaf lettuce, torn into bite-sized pieces
4 cups green leaf lettuce, torn into bite-sized pieces
½ cup slivered mild red onion

1 medium tomato, chopped
1 small green bell pepper, seeded and slivered
½ cup feta cheese, crumbled
2 tablespoons capers (optional)

Combine the vinegar, lemon juice, garlic, salt, dried oregano and pepper in a small bowl. Whisking well, add the olive oil to emulsify. Add olives, cover, and let stand at room temperature for 30 minutes.

In a salad bowl, combine the red and green leaf lettuce, onion, tomato and green bell pepper. Spoon olives over salad and re-whisk dressing. Add dressing to taste and toss. You may not need all of the dressing. Top with crumbled feta and capers if using.

Mint Salad

Here is a light salad that will delight your family and surprise any of your guests wary of mint. Chopping the herb changes the flavor to a delicate spicy green that mixes perfectly with the sharp lemon and salty feta cheese. This beautiful salad, with its variations of green and white, would be lovely as a luncheon dish with grilled lemon chicken. For dinner, serve with Sautéed Chicken Breast with Fresh Orange Salsa (page 170) and Fragrant Barley Casserole (page 254), finishing off the meal with Creeping Cherry Cobbler (page 310).

Betsy Haehl
Alicia Kriewall 2007

6 servings

Dressing

1 lemon, juiced
¼ cup olive oil
¼ cup sesame oil
2 cloves garlic, smashed
1 tablespoon Dijon mustard, or to taste
½ teaspoon salt, or to taste
Pepper to taste

Salad

½ head romaine lettuce, washed and torn into bite-sized pieces
½ head bibb lettuce, washed and torn into bite-sized pieces
1 large bunch mint; all stems removed, leaves finely chopped
6-ounce container Greek Feta cheese

In a small bowl or jar fitted with a tight lid, add the lemon juice, olive and sesame seed oils, garlic, mustard and ½ teaspoon salt and pepper, to taste. Whisk or shake until emulsified. Just prior to serving, remove garlic cloves and shake well. This makes a generous amount of dressing and you may not need all of it for the salad. It will keep in the refrigerator for two weeks.

Place the romaine and bib lettuce in large salad bowl and top with mint. Crumble most of the feta on top of the salad and toss. Add dressing to taste and toss again. Top with the remaining feta.

Summer Heirloom Salad

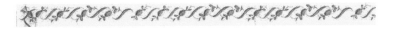

Need a fresh recipe for showcasing your perfect summer heirloom tomatoes besides the expected fresh mozzarella and tomato salads? This is the recipe for you. Irina Sarkisov discovered this salad in *Town & Country* magazine seven years ago and has been serving it with rave reviews ever since. This can be a simple, summery first course by serving it on individual salad plates. Fan out the avocado and tomatoes then top with the fennel, watercress and finally the dressing. Or, serve family style directly with your dinner. But remember: it's necessary to wait until you have ripe summer heirloom tomatoes if you want this salad to turn out perfectly.

Irina Sarkisov
Katya 2006

Serves 6

Salad

2 avocados, thinly sliced
6 (4-by 4-inch) organic heirloom tomatoes, cores removed and sliced into
   ⅛-inch thick slices
2 fennel bulbs, sliced paper thin (reserve in lemon juice and water to
   prevent darkening)
3 bunches baby watercress, cleaned and dried
Salt and cracked black pepper

Champagne Vinaigrette

2 tablespoons champagne vinegar
1 teaspoon Dijon mustard
½ shallot, minced
6 tablespoons extra-virgin olive oil
Salt and pepper to taste

Place sliced avocado around the outside of a serving platter in a circular formation. Fan the tomato around the center. Add shaved fennel directly on top of the tomatoes. Next, place baby watercress in the center and finish the dish with a sprinkling of salt and fresh cracked pepper. Set aside.

In a stainless steel bowl, whisk together the vinegar, mustard and shallot. When the mixture is smooth, slowly add the olive oil while whisking very quickly. Adjust with salt and pepper. Slowly drizzle dressing over salad and serve at once.

Tester's Comments: *I did not have the advantage of wonderful summer tomatoes since I tested this recipe in March. So, to compensate, I used cherry tomatoes, cut in half, then tossed the salad with the dressing allowing the avocado to gently coat the tomatoes, fennel and watercress. I also added a tablespoon more of the vinegar and a pinch of sugar to brighten the flavor of the tomatoes. Even in March, this salad was wonderful.*

Betsy Haehl

Spinach Salad
with Apples and Almonds

This recipe comes from *Tomato Blessings and Radish Teachings*, by Edward Espe Brown, and is truly a gift. Using whole spices that you grind yourself brings out the flavor of this tasty dressing. However, if you do not have a dedicated spice grinder, it is fine to use the pre-ground version. Heating the oil to wilt the greens gives this traditional spinach salad a special flavor.

Sharon Traeger
Alix 2011

Serves 6

½ teaspoon cumin seed
½ teaspoon coriander seed
Juice of one lime (about ¼ cup)
¼ teaspoon salt
1 tablespoon honey
1 apple (Gala, Fuji or Golden Delicious)
¼ cup olive oil
1 clove garlic, minced (optional)
1½ bags (18 ounces) spinach
½ cup slivered almonds, toasted in a 350-degree oven for 8 minutes

To make dressing, toast the cumin and coriander seed in a hot, ungreased skillet until aromatic. Let cool and grind in an electric grinder. Combine with the lime juice, salt and honey; set aside.

Cut the apple into quarters and remove the core. Slice the quarters into thin lengthwise pieces and toss with the dressing.

Put the spinach in a stainless steel, wooden, or ceramic bowl. Heat the olive oil in a small pan until nearly smoking. Stir in garlic, then immediately pour the hot oil over the spinach with one hand while using tongs to toss the spinach with the other. If the spinach is not sufficiently wilted (to your taste) press clumps of it into the hot pan using the tongs. Toss the spinach with the apples. Check and correct the seasonings as needed.

Serve on a platter or individual plates and garnish with the almonds.

Cranberry Spinach Salad

The crunch of the almonds, unique flavor of the sesame seeds, the sweet and sour component of the cranberries and dressing makes this salad a winner. Using pre-washed, packaged spinach makes it a snap to make. This salad would go great with Sautéed Chicken Breasts with Fresh Orange Salsa (page 170). This recipe comes from allrecipes.com.

Trixie Putnam
Matthew 2011
Kent, graduated 8th grade in 1978

12 servings

1 tablespoon butter
¾ cup almonds, slivered
1 pound spinach, rinsed, dried well and torn into bite-sized pieces
1 cup dried cranberries
2 tablespoons sesame seeds, toasted
1 tablespoon poppy seeds
½ cup sugar
2 teaspoons onion, minced
¼ teaspoon paprika
¼ cup white wine vinegar
¼ cup cider vinegar
½ cup vegetable oil

In a medium sauté pan, melt butter over medium heat. Add almonds, stirring, until lightly toasted. Remove from heat, and let cool.

In a large bowl, toss the spinach with the cooled almonds and cranberries.

In a medium bowl, whisk together the sesame seeds, poppy seeds, sugar, onion, paprika, white wine vinegar and cider vinegar. Slowly whisk in the oil until emulsified. Toss with spinach mixture just before serving.   You may not need all of the dressing but it can be stored in the refrigerator for up to 2 weeks.

Wild Rice and Green Pea Salad

This colorful salad makes an ideal side dish in the warm summer months. While it is best eaten right after it is dressed, it still makes a wonderful lunch the next day—especially if you have some leftover chicken or duck to shred into the rice. While we think this salad is a winner, it actually is! Trixie placed the recipe in a food contest and won first prize. Thanks for divulging your secrets to us!

Trixie Putnam
Matthew 2011
Kent graduated 8th grade in 1978

Serves 6

4 tablespoons red wine vinegar
2 tablespoons soy sauce
2 teaspoons honey
½ cup pure olive oil, plus 1 tablespoon for cooking the rice
4 teaspoons sesame oil
1 cup wild rice
¼ teaspoon salt
1 can (14 ounces) chicken broth
2 ½ cups frozen green peas, defrosted
4 celery stocks, diced
6 green onions, sliced thinly
½ cup pecans, toasted in a 350-degree oven for 8 minutes
Salt and pepper to taste

Combine the vinegar, soy sauce, honey, olive oil and sesame oil in a jar with a tight fitting lid or in a small bowl and shake or whisk until emulsified. Can be made up to two days in advance.

Rinse wild rice in cool water. Bring chicken broth to a boil and add the rice, salt and 1 tablespoon olive oil; reduce heat to low, cover and cook for 40 minutes. Cook rice until just done without breaking the kernels. If still hard, cook an additional 5 minutes. Drain, if necessary.

While rice is warm, add the peas, celery, green onions and a small amount of the dressing. Refrigerate until cool. When ready to serve, add dressing to taste (you may not need all of it) and the toasted pecans, coarsely chopped. Salt and pepper to taste.

Corn and Wild Rice Salad

The inspiration for this corn and rice salad was *Judy's Cookbook*. It's also a variation from Wild Rice and Green Pea Salad (page 74), so be sure to read them both and then mix and match to your liking. This is a forgiving recipe that can be adjusted to your family's food preferences. And remember: dress the salad to your taste; you'll possibly want to use a touch more olive oil.

Francesca Purvin
Colton 2011

Serves 12

1 ½ cup uncooked wild rice
3 cups chicken broth
½ teaspoon salt
2 tablespoons olive oil, divided
2 cups fresh corn, about two large ears
1 cup chopped celery
⅔ cup shredded carrot
½ cup chopped sweet yellow onion
¾ cup raisins
¼ cup raspberry or balsamic vinegar
1 tablespoon low-sodium soy sauce
½ teaspoon black pepper
½ teaspoon salt
¾ cup chopped pecans, toasted in a 350-degree oven for 8 minutes

Put rice in a small strainer and rinse well. Place rice, chicken broth, salt and 1 tablespoon olive oil in a medium saucepan and bring to a boil. Reduce heat to low, cover and cook undisturbed until rice is just cooked and grains are not breaking open, about 40 minutes. Drain if necessary, add raw corn and set aside in large bowl to cool and cook the corn.

Combine the cooked rice and corn with the celery, carrots, onions and raisins. Toss well. In a small jar with tight fitting lid, combine the vinegar, soy sauce, remaining tablespoon of olive oil, salt and pepper; shake until well combined. Pour onto rice salad and toss well. Top with toasted pecans and serve.

Mediterranean Pasta Salad

Here is another cold pasta salad that is just as delicious warm. The ingredients are marinated, adding a special flavor to the overall dish. Even if you are serving this dish at room temperature, toss everything while it is warm. It will help to marry the flavor and add depth to the pasta noodle itself.

Irina Sarkisov
Katya 2006

Serves 8 to 10

1 pound uncooked fusilli pasta
1 (7 ounce jar) roasted red peppers, drained and cut into bite-sized pieces
1 (6 ounce jar) marinated artichoke hearts, drained and cut into bite-sized pieces
¼ cup sun dried tomatoes, in oil, cut into strips
¼ cup chopped parsley
¼ cup extra-virgin olive oil
¼ cup pitted and quartered kalamata olives
1 tablespoon plus 1 teaspoon good quality red wine vinegar
½ cup crumbled feta cheese

Cook pasta according to package in a large pot of well-salted water. While pasta is cooking, mix together peppers, artichoke hearts, sun dried tomatoes, parsley, oil, olives and vinegar in a large bowl.

Drain pasta well. Add hot pasta to vegetable mixture, tossing to mix and coat. Salt and pepper to taste. Top with cheese and toss.

Serve warm or at room temperature.

Melon Salad

Tim Conde and his family loved this salad so much that they asked the Animal Kingdom Lodge at Disney World for the recipe. The enthusiastic chefs were happy enough to give it to the Conde family, and we are happy they have shared it with us. It's light, simple to put together and absolutely refreshing during the summer, probably why it is a staple salad at the Lodge.

Tim Conde
Melanie 2011

Serves 10

1 cup plain yogurt
¼ cup port wine
2 tablespoons honey
1 whole cantaloupe, seeded and diced into 1-inch cubes
1 whole honeydew melon, seeded and diced into 1-inch cubes
2 cups seedless watermelon, diced into 1-inch cubes

In a small bowl, combine the port, honey and yogurt. Mix well.

Combine melons in a large bowl; add dressing, toss to coat and serve.

Thai Noodle Chicken Salad

A perfect party dish, this salad can be prepped early in the morning and tossed together right before the guests arrive. Letting the dressing mingle with the noodles before serving helps the dish develop flavor, but wait until you are just ready to serve before adding the vegetables. To create a great vegetarian dish, leave out the chicken and add blanched snow peas, asparagus and broccoli.

Trixie Putnam
Matthew 2011
Kent graduated 8th grade in 1978

Serves 6

12 ounces linguine or fresh Asian noodles
3 tablespoons sesame oil
1 tablespoon peanut oil
6 green onions, chopped
5 garlic cloves, minced
1 tablespoon peeled and minced ginger
¼ cup plus 2 tablespoons honey
¼ cup plus 2 tablespoons creamy peanut butter
¼ cup plus 2 tablespoons soy sauce
4½ tablespoons unseasoned rice vinegar
2½ tablespoons chili-garlic sauce
2 cups mung bean sprouts
1 cup finely shredded carrot
2 green onions, chopped
¼ cup chopped cilantro
2 cups cooked chicken, shredded or cut into bite-sized pieces
¼ cup dry roasted peanuts, coarsely chopped

Bring a large pot of water to a boil. Salt the water to the taste of seawater, approximately 2 tablespoons. Cook the pasta until tender but still firm to the bite, approximately 8 to 10 minutes for dried pasta. Drain. Transfer pasta to large bowl; add 3 tablespoons sesame oil and toss to coat.

While the pasta is cooking, heat peanut oil in a large heavy skillet over medium-high heat. Add the green onions, garlic and ginger and sauté until onions soften, about 2 minutes. Add honey, peanut butter, soy sauce, vinegar and chili-garlic sauce, whisking to blend. Simmer sauce 1 minute. Let sauce cool and pour over pasta; toss to coat. Let the noodles rest with the dressing for at least 30 minutes. Add sprouts, carrots, onions, cilantro and chicken and toss again.

Top with chopped peanuts.

Spicy Sesame Noodle Salad

Cold pasta salads can sometime lack in flavor, but not this one, it has a little bit of everything: crunchy, sweet, spicy and citrus, all in one. It's an excellent dish to serve at a summer buffet and can also be easily adapted with your favorite seasonal vegetables.

Trixie Putnam
Matthew 2011
Kent, graduated 8th grade in 1978

Serves 6

¼ cup fresh lime juice
4 tablespoons Canola oil, divided
3 tablespoons soy sauce
2 tablespoons brown sugar, packed
1 tablespoon sesame oil
1 tablespoon garlic, minced
1 tablespoon grated orange peel
Salt and pepper to taste
2 small Serrano chilies, seeded and minced (or red pepper flakes to taste)
9 ounces green beans, trimmed and cut diagonally into ½-inch pieces
1 (9-ounce) package dried linguine
2 cups peeled and shredded carrots
1 cup thinly sliced green onions

Combine the lime juice, 3 tablespoons of the oil, soy sauce, brown sugar, sesame oil, garlic and orange peel in a small bowl or a jar with a tight fitting lid. Whisk or shake until emulsified. Season to taste with salt and pepper. Let stand 30 minutes to blend flavors.

Cook green beans in a large pot of boiling salted water until tender-crisp, about 3 minutes. Using a slotted spoon, transfer beans to iced water to cool. Drain well and pat dry with paper towels.

Return water to a boil. Add pasta and cook, stirring frequently, until just tender but still firm to bite (about 9 minutes). Drain. Rinse pasta under cold water and drain well. Toss with the remaining tablespoon of oil.

Combine pasta, green beans, carrots and green onions in a large bowl. Add dressing and toss. Season with salt and pepper to taste, cover and chill. Can be made up to 6 six hours ahead of time.

Tester's Comments: *This was delicious. It was zesty with a solid bite of spice. I used the green Serrano peppers instead of red pepper flakes, but if you want a less spicy salad, opt for the pepper flakes. I would absolutely make this again!*

Tamra Tehaney

Thai Chicken Salad

Irina Sarkisov prepares this dish when she is looking for a quick meal for just her daughter and herself. While it is traditionally served family style, with the dressing tossed with all the other ingredients, you could also shake the dressing in a cruet, line individual salad bowls with lettuce, top with the remaining ingredients then pass the dressing at the table. Whichever way the salad is presented, it is definitely one worth serving to your family and friends.

Irina Sarkisov
Katya 2006

Serves 4

¼ cup bottled Thai peanut stir-fry sauce
3 tablespoons fresh lime juice
2 teaspoons freshly grated ginger
½ teaspoon minced garlic

Salad

8 cups loosely packed torn romaine lettuce
2 cups shredded cooked chicken
1½ cups thinly sliced English cucumber
¾ cup shredded carrots
⅓ cup chopped fresh cilantro
¼ cup chopped fresh mint leaves
⅓ cup chopped peanuts

For the dressing, whisk stir-fry sauce, lime juice, ginger and garlic in a large serving bowl until well blended.

Add the lettuce, chicken, cucumber, carrots, cilantro and mint into the bowl with the dressing. Toss to mix, coating well. Sprinkle with peanuts and serve family style.

Tester's Comments: *By using a purchased roasted chicken, packaged romaine lettuce and pre-shredded carrots, this salad came together in less than 15 minutes. For a zippier flavor, we added a few more tablespoons of peanut sauce, a teaspoon of Thai chili sauce and a few extra sprigs of cilantro and mint. It's perfect for a hot summer night meal.*

Betsy Haehl

Chinese Chicken Salad

This recipe is great for a 4th of July picnic, or any other time you need a large quantity of food for a hungry crowd. The dressing and prep work can easily be done ahead of time and thrown together at the last minute, even in an outside location.

Sue Lowe
Taylor Franklin 2002 -2004
Alix Franklin 2010

Serves 8

2 packages chicken-flavored Ramen noodles, flavor packet reserved for dressing
4 tablespoons sesame seeds
1 cup slivered almonds
1 medium head iceberg lettuce, shredded
1 bunch green onions, minced
2 cups cooked chicken, diced or shredded

Dressing

½ cup salad oil
½ cup sesame oil
3 tablespoons sugar
6 tablespoons rice wine vinegar
2 packages Ramen flavoring
Salt and pepper to taste

Preheat the oven to 350 degrees.

86

Break the noodles into small pieces by tapping the noodles in the package with a rubber mallet or meat tenderizer. Place on a tray along with the sesame seeds and almonds; bake until golden, about 8 to 10 minutes, stirring at the halfway point. Let cool. Combine lettuce, green onions, Ramen noodles, sesame seeds, almonds and chicken in a large bowl. Set aside.

To make the dressing, combine salad oil, sesame oil, sugar, vinegar and Ramen flavoring packets in a jar with a tight fitting lid or bowl. Shake or whisk until emulsified. Correct seasonings with salt and pepper; pour over salad; mix and serve.

Tester's Comments: *We tasted the salad immediately after it was completed and it was great. It was even better though after covered and refrigerated for two hours. I served it for dinner with pot stickers on the side. My son who shuns lettuce even liked it.*

Patty Turnquist

The Stanford Shopping Center
Duck Salad

Here is a salad that can be put together with one quick shopping trip to Stanford Shopping Center. Get the marinated duck at Schaubs Meats, the cheese and bread at Oakville Grocery, and everything else at Sigona's. Once the duck is cooked, this salad can be put on the table in under 15 minutes. You can even precook the duck up to an hour ahead, keeping it covered without refrigeration until serving time. This meal is perfect for a fast but elegant dinner before you and your guests head out to a weeknight concert at Villa Montalvo.

Jean Young
Ryan 2012

Serves 4

8 cups mixed spring salad greens
1 pint raspberries
1 small jicama, peeled and cut into thin matchsticks
2 green onions, thinly sliced
4 pomegranate-marinated or plain duck breasts
1 cup candied walnut pieces
1 cup crumbled blue or Roquefort cheese
1 loaf country bread with raisins and nuts
1 bottle of Silver Palette Raspberry Vinaigrette or Berensteins Restaurant Italian Dressing

Preheat oven to 400 degrees.

In a bowl, toss together the mixed spring salad greens, raspberries, jicama and green onions.

Bake duck breast in oven for 20 to 25 minutes or until medium rare. Let duck rest for 5 minutes, remove skin then slice duck at an angle, keeping all the pieces of a breast together.

Toss salad with dressing and lay the sliced duck breast decoratively on top of the salad. Sprinkle with walnuts and cheese. Serve with raisin nut bread and butter or your favorite plain or flavored olive oil. The duck can be served warm or at room temperature.

❧

Testers Comments: *The spicy greens, the sweet raspberries, the crunch of the jicama and the richness of the duck made a great flavor combination. I prefer a milder cheese and used Brie with winning results. I also made my own dressing using ¼ cup raspberry vinegar, 1 tablespoon honey, 2 teaspoons salt and ⅔ cup mild olive oil. Place all ingredients in a jar and shake until blended.*

Mary Pham

Winter Cabbage Salad

The addition of imported prosciutto makes this easy salad extra special. The saltiness of the ham, the bite of the vinegar and the crunch of the cabbage make an excellent combination of flavor. For a bit more zip, add your choice of fresh herbs and a few teaspoons of honey into the dressing.

Mary Pham
David Low 2010

Serves 8

12½ cups cabbage (preferably Savoy), finely shredded
½ cup extra-virgin olive oil
3 tablespoons red wine vinegar
1 tablespoon Dijon mustard, (preferably Maille)
½ teaspoon salt
5 slices prosciutto, cut into julienne
Freshly ground black pepper

For the dressing, place the olive oil, vinegar, mustard and salt in a jar with a tight fitting lid or small bowl and shake or whisk until emulsified. Set aside.

20 to 30 minutes before serving, toss together cabbage and proscuitto. Toss in the dressing. Add black pepper to taste just prior to serving.

Caesar Coleslaw

When the entire Corkery family converges at their Dad's house on Lake Champlain in Vermont, this recipe, adapted from the July 2003 issue of *Bon Appétit*, is always on the menu. Who would think to combine coleslaw with Caesar salad dressing? But it works: the crunch of the cabbage, saltiness of the anchovies and creaminess of the dressing with Parmesan cheese will be the new hit for your 4th of July holiday buffet!

The Corkery Family
Kelsey 2007
Teagan 2009

Serves 14 to 16

1 cup mayonnaise
⅓ cup fresh lemon juice
10 to 12 anchovy fillets, minced
3 garlic cloves, minced
Salt and pepper to taste
1 green cabbage (about 2 ½ pounds), halved, cored and very thinly sliced (about 14 to 16 cups)
16 green onions, thinly sliced
½ to 3/4 cup freshly grated Parmesan cheese

In a small bowl, whisk the mayonnaise, lemon juice, anchovies and garlic. Season dressing to taste with salt and pepper. Place cabbage and green onions in a large bowl. Add dressing and toss to coat. (Can be prepared, up to this point, 1 day ahead.) Cover and refrigerate. Before serving, mix cheese into coleslaw. Transfer to large shallow bowl and serve.

Carrot, Apple, and Fennel Slaw

Yoga, yogurt and wheat germ was Linda Bader's mother's mantra as she raised her family in the 50's, 60's and 70's. Having a mother who was a health food nut way before it was popular made for some interesting dinner conversation amongst the younger generation. Who would have guessed, way back when, that she would be including one of her mom's healthy concoctions into her children's community cookbook! Healthy but delicious! Don't forget to sprinkle a little wheat germ on top for mother's sake.

Linda Bader
Scott Bader 2006
Brett Bader 2012

Serves 4

½ cup plain nonfat yogurt
2 tablespoons white wine vinegar
½ teaspoon celery seeds
¼ teaspoon coarse salt
1 tablespoon freshly chopped tarragon
1 pound carrots, peeled and cut into 3 by ¼ inch matchsticks
1 large fennel bulb, core removed and sliced into ¼ inch half moons
1 Granny Smith apple, unpeeled, cored, and cut into ½ inch wedges
1 teaspoon wheat germ, optional

Place the yogurt, white wine vinegar, celery seeds, salt, and tarragon in a small bowl; whisk to combine.

Place the carrot, fennel and apple in a medium serving bowl. Add the yogurt dressing and toss to combine. Sprinkle optional wheat germ on top and serve.

৵

Breakfast

Our Benedictine Community

The monks teach us through their daily example how to live by the Rule of Saint Benedict. We see them practicing Benedictine values every day, not in a self-conscious display of good manners, but in every interaction they undertake with students, parents, faculty and staff. The following little stories are not remarkable in and of themselves, but together provide a window into the extraordinary community that is Woodside Priory School.

Individuality: Toward the end of the year in his biology class, Father Maurus assigns his sophomores to dissect a fetal pig. One year a student came to him and explained that he didn't think he could do the dissection; it would just make him too queasy. Father Maurus nodded and told the student not to worry, most students become so interested in the science that they are not bothered by the dissection. The day came to distribute the pigs. Father saw that the reluctant student had positioned himself at the end of the line of his classmates who were receiving their pigs, and that as the line became shorter, the student's skin developed an increasingly sickly green pallor. Finally, as he reached the spot where Father Maurus was standing, he was greeted with Father's kind (and face-saving) words: "I am so sorry. I am all out of pigs!"

Integrity: Students with learning disabilities often need to take their final exams apart from their classmates in order to have special accommodations such as word processing or extra time. One student credits Brother Edward for instilling in him, in one sentence, the responsibility of academic integrity and the comfort of Brother Edward's support. On this occasion, Brother Edward led the student to his own office to take an American History final and told him, "When you have finished, please leave your final on my desk, turn off the light, and close the door." And then he left the student to do his final exam. To this day, the student remembers with gratitude and affection Brother Edward's support, trust, and confidence in him.

Spirituality: It is often said that whatever one's religious heritage, being part of the Priory community strengthens one's own personal spirituality. A beloved Dean of Students several years ago left the Priory to move closer to family on the East coast, and in his farewell talk to the students and faculty he related how his understanding of his own Jewish faith was deepened in the years that he worked at this Benedictine school. He said that he came to the Priory on his interview day with much trepidation, having never met monks before, and not knowing what to expect in the hours ahead. He described sitting in the lobby of Founders Hall, waiting for his first interview when a monk in his black habit walked in, nodded, smiled, and sat down in the chair next to him. After what seemed an eternity of silence, Father Martin turned to the obviously nervous applicant, and said, "I bet you didn't expect to be sitting next to a guy in a dress today!" immediately putting the young man at ease. In retrospect, he said in his farewell talk several years hence, it was his first experience in the warm embrace of our Benedictine community, his first step in becoming a "Benedictine Jew."

Hospitality: Several years ago a prospective teacher came during the summer to interview for a teaching position for the following academic year. After spending a long day talking to people on campus, he had a quick dinner in the dining hall before retiring to the guest house for the night. He noted that there were no other people in the dining room, but didn't think too much about it until the next morning when he found the cafeteria closed. At that point, with a sinking feeling in his growling stomach, he realized that naturally the dining hall would not be open on a summer Saturday morning! Just as the hungry fellow began feeding quarters into one of the vending machines near the bookstore, Father Pius rounded the corner on his way to his office. Upon learning the unfortunate man's story, he said, "Oh my good man! Nobody thought to feed you? What kind of Benedictine would I be if I did not give you some breakfast? Follow me!" And with that Father Pius led the fellow up to the monk's dining room and served him a delicious breakfast, and they had a long discussion about art and education and life.

Community: In August, 1955, the Archabbot of the mother abbey in Pannonhalma told the Hungarian Benedictines in America, who were dispersed across the East and Midwest, that they had one year to establish their own community. If they did not find a place and a means of support for themselves in that time, they must go to yet a new country, Brazil, and join a group of their Hungarian brethren who had founded a Benedictine school in São Paulo. Father Egon began driving across the country, visiting bishops and searching for just the right location for a new Benedictine school of the highest academic standards. Over the course of the next ten months he seriously considered and then eliminated sites in Michigan, Indiana, and southern California. Finally, bringing together generous benefactors, Bishop Mitty's hard-won approval, and the blessing of the Archabbot in Pannonhalma, he was able to get word to his Hungarian colleagues: Father Egon was ready to establish a new Beneditine community in Portola Valley, California. On November 11, 1956, the Feast of Saint Martin, the patron saint of the Archabbey of Pannonhalma, Father Egon celebrated Mass in an old ranch house in Portola Valley and marked the end of a long search for a home for a group of displaced monks and the beginning of the Woodside Priory Monastery and School.

Breakfast Burritos

While you do not need a formal recipe to make these burritos, this one provides a wonderful platform to start from. The Taylor family loves their burritos with just salsa, but you can easily add your own favorite condiments.

Virginia Taylor
Geoff 2006
Anna 2007
Katie 2011

Serves 4

8 corn tortillas

4 eggs, beaten with 1 tablespoon of water
1 tablespoon peanut oil
½ cup chopped onion
½ cup chopped cooked meat (chicken, steak, sausage, bacon)
½ teaspoon salt, or to taste
¼ teaspoon cumin
¼ teaspoon Chipotle chili powder, or to taste
¼ cup chopped cherry tomatoes

½ cup grated Cheddar cheese
¼ cup grated Jack cheese

Condiments: salsa, chopped avocado, warm black beans, hot sauce, fresh Mexican cheese (queso ranchero or cotija) crumbled and chopped cilantro.

Cook tortillas by placing one directly on a burner over medium-high heat. Use tongs to flip, leaving the tortilla directly on the flame or electric burner for about 5 seconds. Rotate and turn the tortilla, placing it in various positions on the flame until nicely browned. Set tortillas aside on a microwave-safe plate until all are cooked. Wrap tortillas in a lightly dampened paper towel and set aside.

Heat peanut oil in a 9- to 10-inch skillet over medium-high heat. Add onion, meat, salt, cumin and chili powder; sauté until onions soften, about 3 to 4 minutes. Add tomatoes and eggs; leave to cook until eggs just begin to set. Stir eggs to make a soft curd and remove from heat. Spread eggs evenly in skillet and cover with Cheddar and jack cheese. Cover skillet and let steam until cheese has melted, about 2 minutes.

Keeping the paper towel over the tortillas, reheat tortillas in the microwave at high heat for one minute. Serve warm tortillas with eggs and condiments, letting each guest make his own burrito. Since the corn tortilla is small, just place a strip of eggs down the center, add condiments and roll up jellyroll style without folding over the ends.

Dutch Babies
(Oven Pancake)

These easy to make pancakes puff up in the oven and make a beautiful breakfast presentation. How much they "puff" depends on how long you beat the batter, the ratio of batter to pan size and the consistency of your oven temperature. No matter how they look though, they will become a family favorite! A dusting of powdered sugar and a squeeze of lemon is all they need.

Felice Rebol
Jake 2012

Serves 4

2 tablespoons butter
3 eggs
¾ cup flour
¾ cup milk (non-fat is fine)

Condiments:
Powdered Sugar
Lemon Wedges
Fresh berries, washed and sliced
Syrup
Jam

Preheat oven to 425 degrees.

Prepare and set out the powdered sugar, lemon, berries, syrup and jam on the table so they are ready when the pancakes come out of the oven.

Place butter in a 9 x 14-inch baking dish. Place dish in oven to melt butter, about 1 to 2 minutes, being careful not to burn.

In a mixer, beat eggs about 30 seconds. Continue beating eggs on low speed while alternately adding flour and milk until mixed.

Pour batter into prepared hot dish. Batter should cover the bottom of the dish and fill it ¼- to ½-inch high. Do not add too much batter or pancake will not puff up and will taste "doughy".

You can scale this recipe up or down successfully if you remember to fill the pan only ¼- to ½-inch high. The butter should be just enough to cover the bottom of the pan. The amount of butter does not need to increase proportionally to the other ingredients, it just needs to cover the bottom of your dish.

Bake 12 to 15 minutes. Pancake will puff up in the oven.

Cut, serve and eat immediately!

Cottage Cheese Griddlecakes

A family favorite in the Davison household, this recipe was adapted from the 12th edition of *The Fannie Farmer Cookbook*. For those of you interested in high protein, low carbohydrate breakfasts, this is the perfect substitute for traditional pancakes. Be sure to gently turn these tender pancakes, and let them cook a little longer than you would a traditional pancake.

Wayne and Cindy Davison
Amanda 2000
Andy 2008

Makes about 12 griddlecakes

1 cup low-fat cottage cheese
3 large eggs, well beaten
2 tablespoons melted butter
1 teaspoon orange peel
½ teaspoon orange extract
3 teaspoons sugar
½ cup white flour
½ teaspoon salt
½ teaspoon powdered ginger

Condiments:
Warm maple syrup
Orange marmalade
Powdered sugar

Combine the cottage cheese, eggs, melted butter, orange peel, orange extract and sugar; stir until well mixed. Fold in the flour, salt and ginger; mix just enough to blend together.

Prepare a griddle or frying pan over medium heat. Grease hot griddle with butter or oil and wipe clean with a paper towel, or lightly spray with cooking spray. Drop large spoonfuls of batter onto prepared griddle and cook on one side until lightly browned. Turn gently with a spatula and cook the other side until browned and fully cooked.

Serve immediately with warmed maple syrup or orange marmalade. Sprinkle with powdered sugar

Tester's Comments: *We were tempted to add a little more orange extract or ginger for a more pronounced flavor but they were great just the way they were!*

Liz Bellock

Corn Flapjacks

If you like the crunch of cornmeal, you will be sure to like these pancakes. Resting the batter overnight takes a bit of the crunch out and also makes a more tender pancake. Whether you choose crunchy or not so crunchy, be sure to rest the batter for at least two hours.

Liz Ditz
Allison Littlefield 2007

Serves 4

1⅓ cups white corn meal
1¼ teaspoon salt
½ teaspoon baking soda
¼ cup all-purpose flour
¼ cup butter, cut into small dice and chilled
2 eggs
2 cups buttermilk
Vegetable oil

Condiments:
Butter
Warm maple syrup

Mix together corn meal, salt, baking soda, and flour in a medium-sized bowl or in the bowl of a food processor. Cut in butter until pieces are about the size of small pellets or pulse the butter in 5 or 6 times.

Beat eggs lightly and add buttermilk. Add egg/buttermilk mixture to dry ingredients and stir briefly to mix. Alternately, with your food processor running, pour in the wet ingredients and process until just combined. Allow batter to rest; pancakes are best when the batter rests several hours or overnight.

Prepare the griddle: Heat your griddle or pan over medium-high heat. Pour a small amount of oil onto your cooking surface and wipe with a paper towel until pan is thinly coated. Test by spritzing a few drops of water onto the griddle. If it just boils, it needs to be hotter; if it vaporizes, let it cool a bit; the drops should bounce and sputter.

Stir batter prior to ladling, as it tends to separate.

Ladle batter onto hot griddle; bubbles will appear on the pancake. Cook until bubbles are set; then flip the pancake over. The second side will take half as long as the first.

Serve hot off the griddle with plenty of butter and warm maple syrup.

Breakfast Crepes

This is the Taylor kid's favorite breakfast, hands down! While time consuming, this recipe is not difficult. The key to creating a thin crepe is a good quality, small, nonstick sauté pan, the correct temperature and the proper amount of batter. Once the batter is poured into the pan and swirled around, pour out any excess to avoid thick crepes. This batter is fool proof and can also be used for desserts.

Virginia Taylor
Geoff 2006
Anna 2007
Katie 2011

Makes 32 crepes

1 cup all-purpose flour
½ cup cake flour
6 tablespoons sugar
½ teaspoon salt
4 eggs, beaten
2 ½ cups milk
½ cup butter, melted
1 teaspoon vanilla
Butter for cooking
Condiments: jams of your choice, powdered sugar, warm maple syrup, peanut butter, bananas, Nutella, dulce de leche

In the bowl of your food processor, place the all-purpose flour, cake flour, sugar and salt; process until combined. In a 4-cup measuring bowl with pouring spout, mix the eggs, milk, butter and vanilla. Through the feed tube of the processor, add the wet ingredients to the dry while the motor is running. Once mixed, pour the blended crepe mixture back into the

108

measuring bowl. It will be the consistency of heavy cream. If possible, let rest for 1 hour. This will create a more tender crepe.

Heat your 6-inch nonstick skillet, with rounded sides, over medium heat. Swipe a stick of butter around the pan and immediately pour in about 2 to 3 tablespoons of batter. Quickly tip the pan to evenly distribute the batter, pouring out excess if there is any. Cook on one side until brown and well cooked, lift up the edge of your crepe with a butter knife and with your fingers, grab the edge of the crepe and flip it over to cook for an additional 5 to 10 seconds. Flip onto a cutting board and make another crepe with the remaining batter, swirling the butter around the skillet about every third or fourth crepe. While that crepe is cooking, quickly fill the crepe on the cutting board with about 3 teaspoons of jam, spreading it evenly over the surface. Roll the crepe up and place in a 200-degree oven until the remaining crepes are done. Flip the next crepe and turn out onto your cutting board and repeat until all crepes are done. Sprinkle the top with powdered sugar and ring the breakfast bell!

Tester's Comments: *I had remaining batter which I used that night as dessert. I filled the crepes with chocolate fondue and orange sections with the white pith removed. It was a hit!*

Suzanne Frappier

Stuffed French Toast

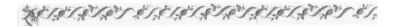

Here is a convenient way to make French toast without hovering over the stove. The bread is cubed, placed in an ovenproof dish, covered with a sweetened egg/milk mixture and baked. This recipes calls for the addition of cream cheese but is just as delicious without. Add a side of bacon or sausage and fruit to create a wonderful holiday brunch. Please note that the dish must rest for at least one hour before baking, but can be made the day before and popped into the oven after bringing back to room temperature.

Lisa Plain
Hap 2006
Alex 2008

Serves 10

1 pound good quality (whole loaf) day-old white bread, cubed
8-ounce package cream cheese, cubed (easier if chilled or even lightly
   frozen)
12 large eggs
1½ cups milk
½ cup maple syrup, plus extra for serving

Grease a 13 x 9-inch baking dish with butter or cooking spray.

Spread half of the bread into the prepared pan. Sprinkle half of the cubed cream cheese over the bread. Repeat the layers of bread and cream cheese.

Whisk eggs, milk and maple syrup together, mixing well. Pour over bread and cheese. Cover and refrigerate for at least one hour or overnight. Bring to room temperature before baking.

Bake in a preheated 350-degree oven for 30 to 40 minutes, or until a knife inserted in the middle remains clean. Let stand for 15 minutes before serving.

Serve with the additional warmed maple syrup.

Breakfast Soufflé with Bacon

Kelly Pettit's mother, Marilyn Morrow, shares her breakfast recipe that she usually serves to her family on Christmas morning for brunch. The great thing about this soufflé is that it can easily be made the night before and customized to your family's taste buds. Just add your favorite veggies or melting cheeses into the mix! To make a perfect morning meal, serve with fruit and Banana Oatmeal Bread (page 304) or Almond Cake (page 296).

Kelly Pettit
Angela 2008

Serves 8

9 slices white bread, cubed in 1-inch squares
¾ pound Swiss cheese, grated
¾ pound Monterey Jack cheese, grated
2 pounds bacon or sausage, cooked and crumbled
3 cups sliced mushrooms, salted and sautéed until brown in butter (optional)
2 green onions, thinly sliced (optional)
6 eggs
3 cups milk
¾ teaspoon dried mustard
¾ teaspoon salt
¾ teaspoon onion salt
¾ teaspoon Worcestershire sauce

Prepare 9 x 13-inch pan with butter.

Place cubed bread in prepared pan. Mix cheese, bacon or sausage, and mushrooms and onions if desired. Distribute evenly over the bread. In a blender, mix the eggs, milk, mustard, salt, onion salt and Worcestershire sauce, and pour over the bread and cheese. Refrigerate covered overnight.

In the morning preheat the oven to 350 degrees. Bake for 40 to 60 minutes, or just until browned and set.

Tester's Comments: *This recipe was extremely easy, and I always love a recipe I can make the day before. I would purchase pre-shredded cheeses to save on the prep time.*

Patty Turnquist

Cinnamon Rolls

Whether you're looking for a gooey, delicious addition to a Sunday brunch, or just an easy, yummy treat for a school morning, these cinnamon rolls are sure to hit the spot. Add walnuts for a nice crunch, or top with vanilla frosting and dust with cinnamon for extra sweetness!

Pamela Martinson
Marisa 2010

Makes 8 rolls

3 tablespoons packed brown sugar, divided
2 tablespoons butter, plus additional for preparing pan
1½ tablespoons cinnamon
1 tablespoon sugar
1 loaf frozen bread dough
2 tablespoons melted butter

Thaw bread dough overnight in refrigerator.

Preheat oven to 350 degrees. Prepare an 8- or 9-inch round cake pan with butter; cover bottom of cake pan with 2 tablespoons brown sugar and dot with butter.

Mix together the cinnamon, sugar and remaining 1 tablespoon of brown sugar. Roll dough into a large rectangle about 9 x 14-inches. Brush butter on dough and sprinkle with cinnamon and sugar mixture.

Roll the dough up lengthwise to form one long jelly roll log. Using a sharp knife, cut into 8 slices.

Arrange slices in pan, sides touching. Let rise in a warm place for about 1 hour until about doubled in size. Rolls can also be made up to this point the day before and left to rise in the refrigerator. Place directly into the oven from the refrigerator.

Bake in preheated oven for 15 to 20 minutes.

Flip rolls out of pan onto a serving plate with the brown sugar side up. Serve warm.

Tester's Comments: *This recipe was simple, straightforward and delicious. It definitely helps to roll the dough out on a floured surface. If you are not serving this as a midday brunch dish, I would recommend preparing the rolls the night before, letting them rise in the refrigerator overnight and then pop them in the oven the next morning. Otherwise, you will have to wait one hour for the dough to rise.*

Susan Dennis

Yummy Cinnamon Sugar Rolls

Here is another version of cinnamon rolls, which calls for the dough to be made in a bread machine instead of purchasing it pre-made. The gooey cinnamon rolls are a favorite of the Trudelle family children, who ask for a batch on their birthday to share at school with their friends. The frosting is not necessary, but sweetens up the traditional bread dough. You can try both versions, mixing and matching the dough, frosting and cinnamon sugar filling of each recipe until you find your favorite.

Sylvia Trudelle
Steve 2000
Peter 2003
Laura 2005
Chrissa 2007
Marie 2010

Makes 24

Dough

1⅓ cups of warm water
2 eggs
3 tablespoons sugar
2 teaspoons salt
4 cups bread flour
6 tablespoons of butter
2 ½ teaspoons yeast

Filling

5 tablespoons melted butter, divided
6 tablespoons sugar, divided
2 tablespoons of ground cinnamon
Optional Additions:
½ cup golden raisins
½ cup chopped walnuts
2 tablespoons butter, melted

Frosting

1 cup powdered sugar
1 to 2 tablespoons milk

Place the water, eggs, sugar, salt, flour and butter into the box of your bread machine. Add yeast in the proper location for your machine. If the machine does not have a yeast box, add yeast first, before all other ingredients. Set the bread machine on a manual "dough only" setting.

Preheat oven to 400 degrees.

Take the completed dough from the container and divide in half. Liberally flour a work surface and roll each half of dough into an approximate 16 x 12-inch rectangle. Brush with 2 ½ tablespoons of melted butter. Mix the sugar and cinnamon and divide in half, sprinkling one half evenly over each rectangle of dough. Sprinkle with optional raisins and nuts. Roll the dough jellyroll style, and cut into 12 slices approximately 1 inch wide. Repeat with the other half of dough.

Prepare muffin tins with butter or cooking spray. Place each slice into the prepared tins, cover and let rise in a warm place about 35 to 40 minutes. Bake for 20 to 30 minutes in the preheated oven.

(continued)

While the cinnamon rolls are cooking, make the frosting. Place the powdered sugar in a bowl and stir while adding the milk. Add just enough milk to get a glaze consistency.

When the rolls are done, brush with melted butter (optional) while hot. Cool in tins for 5 minutes, spoon on the frosting and let rest for 5 more minutes. Serve warm or at room temperature. It's best to eat the rolls the same day, however, they do freeze nicely.

Tester's Comments: *If desired, the dough can be baked while still in the jellyroll stage. Simply form the roll into a crescent and bake at 400 degrees for 20 to 25 minutes, or until a wooden stick inserted in the center comes out clean.*

Margaret Herzen

Pumpkin Chocolate Chip Muffins

For a special Halloween treat, consider making these sweets for your monsters and goblins. The addition of canned pumpkin and sweet chocolate chips turns a simple muffin recipe into a special treat—great for before or after school!

Valerie Wookey
Sarah 2010
Jack 2012

Makes about 36 mini muffins

2 cups flour
1 cup sugar
1 teaspoon baking soda
1 teaspoon baking power
1 cup butter, melted
2 eggs
¾ cup canned pumpkin
1 cup chocolate chips

Preheat oven to 350 degrees. Prepare mini muffin tins with butter or cooking spray.

In a bowl, combine flour, sugar, baking soda and baking powder. In a separate bowl, mix butter, eggs, pumpkin and chocolate chips. Add in the flour mixture and combine well. Spoon batter evenly into mini muffin pans, and bake for about 12 to 15 minutes. Let cool before removing from pan.

Southern Sour Cream Coffee Cake

This coffee cake was made for the first meeting of the cookbook committee and received rave reviews. The moist but light cake, layered with a sweet, crunchy topping, is just what we dreamed of for a perfect morning treat. We felt this recipe set the stage for the many other wonderful recipes to follow.

Valerie Wookey
Sarah 2010
Jack 2012

Serves 12

2 cups flour
1 teaspoon baking powder
1 teaspoon baking soda
1 cup butter, softened
1 cup sugar
3 eggs
½ cup sour cream

Topping

1 cup brown sugar
2 tablespoons flour
3 tablespoons melted butter
1 cup pecans, chopped

Preheat oven to 350 degrees. Prepare a standard angel food cake pan or large loaf pan with butter and flour.

Mix together flour, baking powder and baking soda in a medium-sized bowl. Set aside. In the bowl of a mixer or in a food processor, cream together butter and sugar. Add eggs one at a time, then the sour cream. Gradually add in flour mixture and beat for 10 minutes with a mixer or for 5 minutes with a food processor.

Mix together brown sugar, flour, butter and pecans in a small bowl.

Pour ½ of batter into the pan of your choice. Sprinkle with half of the brown sugar mixture. Pour the rest of the batter on top. Sprinkle with remaining half of the brown sugar mixture.

Bake at 350 degrees for about 45 minutes, or until a knife inserted in the middle comes out clean. Freezes well.

Tester's Comments: *I did not have an angel food pan so I prepared this cake in a Bundt pan. I carefully prepared the pan with butter and flour to prevent any topping from sticking in the ridges of the pan. I then placed a small portion of the batter in the bottom of the pan and placed half of the topping over the batter. Next, I covered the topping with a thin layer of batter then placed the rest of the topping on. I then covered that layer with the remaining batter (almost half of the batter) to cover the topping completely. Let the cake rest in the pan until cool before removing.*

Virginia Taylor

Fish

A Little Local History

Portola Valley is named to commemorate the intrepid Spanish explorer Gaspar de Portolá, who led an overland expedition from San Diego to San Francisco in the fall of 1769. The expedition spent several days camped near Montara in order to allow Portolá to recover from an illness. Exploration parties, led by guides from local Indian settlements, discovered that they were between the Pacific Ocean and a great inland sea, which they identified as the Bay of San Francisco. On their return march south, the expedition camped on the north bank of San Francisquito Creek across from a giant redwood tree they dubbed El Palo Alto. They followed a trail that led through what is now Redwood City and Woodside, so it is likely that they walked through the lovely valley that now bears Portolá's name.

Another local name, Corte de Madera, means "timber choppings," and refers to the redwoods that were logged to build the Pueblo of San José and the Mission Santa Clara. By the 1830's, a drayage road (arrastradero) led from the local forests to the bay, where boats could transport the lumber to the southern settlements. In 1883, Andrew S. Hallidie, the inventor of the San Francisco cable car, purchased land in Portola Valley and even built an aerial tramway that was suspended by an overhead cable from his estate to the top of a nearby mountain.

The bell that stands next to Founders' Hall was installed in the 1980's as a reminder that the history of the land that is now Woodside Priory School includes people and events from the pre-Columbian, Spanish, Californio and American eras of our state. It is one of the commemorative bells that were placed in 1906 along the original El Camino Real, "the Royal Road," that stretched from mission to mission, from Mexico to Sonoma. The dates "1796 & 1906" are printed together on the bell—1796 referring to the founding of the first California mission in San Diego, and 1906 referring to the placement of the first El Camino bell in Los Angeles.

Halibut
with Grapefruit and Blood Orange Sauce

Felice Rebol found this award-winning recipe in the newspaper and was happy to find a recipe that uses her favorite citrus fruits. The tangy-sweet sauce pairs nicely with the mild flavor of the halibut. The addition of fresh orange and grapefruit sections as a garnish rounds out this unusual dish.

Felice Rebol
Jake Koval 2012

Serves 4

1 pound halibut steaks
2 tablespoons olive oil
1 cup fresh red grapefruit juice (divided), about 2 grapefruits
½ teaspoon minced fresh thyme
1 clove garlic, minced
Salt and pepper to taste
¼ cup butter (divided)
1 teaspoon minced shallot
½ cup blood orange juice, about 2 oranges
1 tablespoon chives, cut into 1-inch pieces
½ grapefruit in sections, white pith removed, cut into small pieces
2 blood oranges in sections, white pith removed, cut into small pieces

Rinse halibut steaks under running water and pat dry with paper towels. Place fish in a separate dish just large enough to hold them. In a small bowl, combine olive oil, ½ cup grapefruit juice, thyme and garlic. Add salt and pepper to taste. Pour mixture over fish. Cover and marinate for 15 to 20 minutes in the refrigerator.

Preheat oven to 400 degrees. Lightly butter or coat a baking dish with vegetable spray.

Take fish out of marinade and place in prepared baking dish. Dot fish with ½ tablespoon of butter; bake for 15 minutes, basting once or twice with butter and pan juices.

While fish is baking, prepare the sauce.

Heat ½ tablespoon butter in a small saucepan until melted. Stir in shallot and sauté over low heat until just tender, about 1 minute. Stir in remaining ½ cup grapefruit juice and blood orange juice and bring to a boil. Reduce heat to a simmer and cook until juice is reduced to ¼ cup, about 20 minutes. Whisk remaining cold butter into sauce, bit by bit, until sauce thickens slightly. Salt and pepper to taste.

When fish is done, remove from the oven and place on serving plates. Sprinkle lightly with salt. Spoon citrus sauce over top and garnish with a sprinkle of chives and cut fruit. Use fresh fruit sparingly as it can overwhelm the halibut.

Braised Halibut
in Saffron Infused Broth

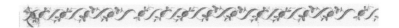

This recipe, adapted from Judy Roger's *Zuni Café* cookbook, is one of the Taylor family staples. The browned fennel, slow-cooked onion and garlic plus the tomatoes and saffron impart the broth with an unforgettable flavor. Serve this with ciabatta bread cut in half, broiled or grilled then brushed with olive oil and sprinkled with coarse salt. Dipping the bread in the broth is just heavenly.

Virginia Taylor
Geoff 2006
Anna 2007
Katie 2011

Serves 4

4 halibut filets, about six ounces each
Salt
½ cup mild tasting extra-virgin olive oil
1 medium fennel bulb, trimmed and cut into ½-inch slices
¾ cup chopped onion
¾ cup dry white wine
1 clove garlic, chopped
Pinch of chili flakes
Healthy pinch of saffron
1 cup peeled, seeded and chopped tomatoes
1 cup cubed Yukon Gold potatoes, cooked al dente, salted and coated with olive oil
¾ cup ½-inch sliced green beans, cooked (or frozen peas defrosted)
2 cups fish broth or chicken stock (canned is fine)

Season the fish with the salt, 4 to 12 hours in advance if possible.

128

Heat two tablespoons of oil in a 12-inch skillet. Add the fennel and cook over medium heat until golden, about three minutes per side. Reduce the heat and add the onions, another tablespoon or two of oil and a few pinches of salt. Cook gently for about 10 minutes, stirring the onion and turning the pieces of fennel as needed. Continue to brown the fennel and slow cook the onions by keeping the fennel in the center of the pan and sautéing the onion on the outer edge of the pan. The salt, the low flame and the stirring should coax the onions to sweat their water without browning. Cut each piece of fennel into two or three slices (I do this right in the pan).

Add the white wine and raise the heat to medium-high, allowing the broth to boil briefly; add the garlic, chili flakes and saffron. Lower heat and bring to a quiet simmer; cook for about 5 minutes. Add the tomato and cook an additional 2 minutes. Add the fish stock, bring to a simmer on medium heat and correct for seasonings. Set aside off the heat.

For the fish, heat 1 tablespoon or so of oil in a 10-inch skillet over medium heat. When the oil starts to smoke, arrange the fish in the pan (they should sizzle on contact). Cook until a nice crust is developed then place the halibut raw side down in the broth. Strew on the potatoes and beans or peas. This can all be done in advance, even refrigerated.

To finish, start your broiler and reheat the broth to a simmer. Place the pan under the broiler and broil for 3 to 5 minutes to finish cooking the fish and to brown the potatoes.

Recipe Note: Be adventurous with this dish. Use cooked cannelini beans instead of potatoes, baby artichokes for the vegetable or even throw in a few tablespoons of romesco sauce for a true taste sensation. It is wonderful served with a dollop of aioli.

129

Almond Crusted Halibut with Beurre Blanc

Trixie Putnam uses this recipe, from allrecipes.com, when she wants to impress her guests. The crunchy almond topping with the flaky halibut is made elegant with the addition of the butter sauce. This traditional French sauce is more forgiving by the adding of cream to the base. You can keep the sauce warm by placing it into a thermos until needed. For a lighter entrée, skip the sauce.

Trixie Putnam
Matthew 2011
Kent Putnam graduated 8th grade in 1978

Serves 6

⅓ cup dry white wine
2 tablespoons cider vinegar
2 tablespoons minced shallots
1 sprig fresh thyme
1 bay leaf
⅓ cup heavy cream
10 tablespoons unsalted butter, chilled and cut into tablespoon-sized pieces
3 tablespoons chopped fresh chives
2 teaspoons fresh lemon juice
Salt and pepper to taste
6 (6-ounce) halibut fillets
2 tablespoons vegetable oil
1 tablespoon unsalted butter
¼ cup fresh bread crumbs
⅔ cup minced blanched almonds
1 tablespoon unsalted butter, melted
1 egg, lightly beaten

Make beurre blanc: Combine wine, vinegar, shallots, thyme and bay leaf in a small saucepan over medium heat. Boil until liquid has almost evaporated. Stir in cream and boil until liquid is reduced by half; decrease heat to low. Whisk in butter, 1 piece at a time, adding each new piece before previous one has incorporated completely into the sauce. Do not allow sauce to simmer or it may separate.

Strain sauce through a fine sieve into a heat proof bowl. Stir in chives, lemon juice, salt and pepper. Keep warm by setting bowl in a larger container of hot water.

Preheat oven on broiler setting. Pat halibut fillets dry, and season with salt and pepper.

Heat oil and 1 tablespoon butter in a large skillet over medium-high heat. Sauté halibut fillets for 2 to 3 minutes on each side, or until lightly browned, and almost cooked through. Transfer to a baking sheet and cool 5 minutes. In a small bowl, stir together bread crumbs, almonds and 1 tablespoon melted butter. Brush tops of fillets with egg, and spread with almond mixture.

Broil fillets 1 to 2 minutes, or until browned and cooked through. Watch closely—every broiler has its own personality! Place fillets on individual plates, and top with beurre blanc.

Tester's Comments: *Instead of making the sauce completely ahead of time, stop after reducing cream and before adding the butter. As the halibut is broiling, add the butter to finish the sauce, making sure to keep an eye on the broiling fish. I only added half the butter and it was still wonderful.*

Amy Magnuson

Escalopes de Saumon
au Citron Vert
(Salmon in Lime Sauce)

One of Margaret Herzen's favorite ways of preparing salmon comes from a cooking class she took years ago at the now gone Charlotte Combe Cooking School on Woodside Road in Redwood City. (Some may even recognize it!) The citrus lime sauce perfectly complements the strong flavor of the salmon. Serve with a side of grilled vegetables for a refreshing, light evening dinner during the summer months.

Margaret Herzen
Elena 2003
Juliana 2007

Serves 6

4 limes
6 (4 to 6-ounce) salmon fillets, skinned and pin bones removed
Salt and freshly ground pepper
Juice of 1 lime
4 tablespoons olive oil
1 lime
⅓ cup dry vermouth
2 cups good quality fish stock (frozen Perfect Additions)
⅓ cup of cream
2 tablespoons butter

Using a sharp paring knife, cut off the green peel of the 4 limes, trying not to remove any of the white pith. Cut into julienne strips. Put in a small pan, cover with cold water and bring to a boil. Drain at once and cool in cold water, then dry with paper towel and set aside. Cut the flesh of the 4 limes into segments without the membrane by first removing all the white pith from the lime and then, with your paring knife, removing each segment of the lime between the membrane. Set aside.

Preheat oven to 250 degrees. Season salmon with salt, pepper and lime and set aside for 10 minutes. Lightly brush salmon with 2 tablespoons olive oil. Heat a 12-inch cast iron pan over medium-high heat. Add 2 tablespoons of olive oil. When butter begins to sizzle, add the salmon and cook undisturbed for 3 minutes. Turn salmon, add lime zest and cook for another 2 minutes. Place fish on an ovenproof plate and put in warming oven while you finish the sauce.

Add vermouth to the cast iron pan with the lime zest and reduce, over medium-high heat, by half. Add the fish stock and reduce again by half. Add lime segments and reduce for another 5 minutes over medium heat. Add cream, return to a simmer, and cook for a few more minutes to reduce slightly. Whisk in the butter, 1 tablespoon at a time, into the sauce. Season to taste with salt and pepper.

Pour the sauce over the salmon fillets and serve.

Salmon with Fresh Sorrel

Francesca and Jeff Purvin chose this dish for their wedding dinner entrée. We can see why: The tart, brilliant green sauce looks and tastes wonderful with the rich salmon. The technique of making the sorrel butter, then incorporating it into the sauce, helps maintain the sorrel's vibrant apple green color, which our tester, Mary Pham, was determined to keep.

Jeff and Francesca Purvin
Colton 2011

Serves 6

3 cups fresh sorrel
4 tablespoons unsalted butter
½ cup white wine
¼ cup dry vermouth
½ cup fish stock (frozen Perfect Additions)
2 shallots, minced
4 tablespoons crème fraîche
Salt to taste
2 tablespoons light olive oil
6 (6-ounce) salmon fillets, pin bones removed and salted two hours before cooking

Make sorrel butter by placing sorrel in the food processor and pulsing until chopped. Add butter and process until well incorporated. Remove to a small bowl, cover but do not refrigerate.

Mix together wine, vermouth, fish stock and shallots in a saucepan. Over medium heat, reduce mixture to ¼ cup. Whisk in crème fraîche and reduce heat to the lowest setting while preparing the salmon.

Heat a sauté pan over medium-high heat, add oil and, right before the smoking point, add salmon fillets, searing well on one side, about 3 minutes. As the salmon is searing, finish the sauce by turning up the heat and whisking in the sorrel butter, a bit at a time, until incorporated but not melted. Set aside in warm spot.

Turn the fillet after it is well browned on one side and cook on the other side until still pink in the center, about another 2 minutes. Remove from heat onto warmed serving plates and top with the sauce. Or, plate the sauce first and then place the salmon on top of the sauce.

Seared Salmon
on Black Bean and Roast Banana Mash
with Coconut-Serrano Broth

This unique recipe was developed by Stephan Pyles, the true creator of Southwestern cuisine. It has many steps but all can be done ahead of time making it perfect for a dinner party. Virginia Taylor taught this as an appetizer at one of her cooking classes to benefit The Priory, but it definitely can be served as a main course. Add the Roasted Red Pepper Soup (page 52) for an elegant dinner party menu!

Virginia Taylor
Geoff 2006
Anna 2007
Katie 2011

Serves 6

Salmon Fillets

6 salmon fillets (3 to 6 ounces each)
½ cup soy sauce
½ cup lightly packed brown sugar
2 tablespoons olive oil

Black Bean and Roast Banana Mash

1 cup black beans, soaked overnight (or 2 cups canned)
4 cups chicken or vegetable stock
2 bananas
2 tablespoons olive oil
½ small onion, finely diced
2 cloves garlic, peeled and minced

136

1 tablespoon tomato paste
2 tablespoons chili powder
1 tablespoon lime juice
1 tablespoon butter
Salt to taste

Coconut-Serrano Broth

1 tablespoon olive oil
½ medium carrot, peeled and roughly chopped
1 stalk celery, chopped
½ medium onion, chopped
3 serranos, seeded and chopped
½ teaspoon ground cumin
2 stalks lemon grass, chopped
2 kaffir lime leaves
1 cup Sherry
1 (14 ounce can) coconut milk
1 cup chicken stock
2 teaspoons brown sugar
Dash of fish sauce
1 cup cilantro leaves
½ cup basil leaves
Salt to taste

Mango Tortilla Salad

4 corn tortillas, cut into strips
Vegetable oil for frying
Juice of 4 limes
½ cup olive oil
Salt to taste
½ jicama, peeled and julienned
1 mango, peeled and julienned
½ red pepper, julienned
¼ cup cilantro leaves

(continued)

Remove the pin bones and black flesh from the salmon fillet. In a dish, just large enough to hold the fillets, combine the soy sauce and brown sugar; whisk until sugar has melted into the soy sauce. Add the salmon and marinate for at least 20 minutes but no more than 45.

Black Bean and Roast Banana Mash: Preheat oven to 350 degrees.

In a saucepan, combine the black beans with the stock and cook over low heat until the beans are soft, 1 to 1½ hours or use 2 cups of rinsed canned black beans.

Roast the bananas in their skins in the preheated oven until the fruit is soft and the skins are black, about 15 minutes.

Heat the olive oil in a sauté pan over medium-high heat until lightly smoking; add the onion and garlic and sauté for 2 minutes. Add the tomato paste and stir constantly for 2 minutes. Add the chili powder and continue cooking for an additional 2 minutes. Remove from heat and set aside.

Place the beans, the bananas (peeled) and the onion mixture in a food processor and blend with the butter and lime juice until smooth, about 1 minute. If too thick (should be the consistency of mashed potatoes) add the bean cooking liquid or water to get the mash to the proper consistency. Salt to taste and set aside (can be made up to 2 days in advance).

Coconut-Serrano Broth: Heat the olive oil in a large saucepan over medium-high heat. Sauté the carrot, celery and onion for 3 minutes until the onion is translucent. Add the serranos, cumin, lemongrass and the lime leaves; continue to sauté for 1 minute more.

Deglaze the pan with the sherry and reduce to a glaze. Add the coconut milk and broth; bring to a boil. Reduce the heat and simmer for 5 minutes. Add the sugar and the dash of fish sauce. Let cool and then place in blender and purée until smooth, about 1 minute. Strain the broth through a fine sieve. Place back into a saucepan and reheat. Season to taste with salt. Tie the cilantro and basil together with a piece of twine (it will be easier to remove at the end) and steep in the warm broth until ready to use.

Tortilla and Mango Salad:
Heat one inch of vegetable oil in a medium saucepan until lightly smoking. Fry the tortillas in batches until crisp. Remove from oil and drain on paper towels, salting while hot.

Place the lime juice in a glass jar. Add oil and a pinch of salt. Shake until emulsified. Right before serving, combine the jicama, mango, red bell pepper, tortilla strips and cilantro in a large bowl and toss with the vinaigrette.

Salmon Fillets:
Heat the olive oil in a large skillet over high heat until lightly smoking. Remove the pan from the heat, gently place the salmon, patted dry of it's marinade in the pan and return to the heat. Sear the salmon for about 2 minutes. Turn the salmon over and continue to sear on the other side, about 2 minutes longer for medium rare.

To serve, remove the cilantro and basil from the broth and squeeze broth out of herbs, discard. Reheat the broth and place about ¼ cup of the broth in a wide, shallow soup bowl. Reheat the black bean and roasted banana mash in a microwave until hot and place a good dollop in the center of the bowl. Place the salmon on the mash and top with a small handful of the mango-tortilla salad and serve.

Tester's Comments: *Please do not be put off by the length of this recipe—the end result is absolutely worth it. I am not a big fan of black beans but I was pleasantly surprised how the roasted bananas transformed their flavor. I would have never dreamed to put this combination together but it works and my guests and family loved it.*

Trixie Putnam

Red Snapper
with Eggplant, Tomatoes and Lemon

This dish known as "Ongree" in Arabic, and was given to us by Marian Scheuer Sofaer, whose husband's family is Iraqi and Jewish. Ongree is also knows as "Salona" by the Hindawis and commonly called "Sweet and Sour Fish." This recipe revived the family tradition of serving ongree after trying a delicious version made by the great Iraqi Jewish cooks Hanna and David Hindawi of Berkeley. The Sofaer family's life in Rangoon, Calcutta and Bombay has influenced the taste of this recipe but it is the extraordinary touches of Raphael's ('08) Bombay-born grandmother, Mozelle, which makes this the perfect ongree.

Marian Scheuer Sofaer
Raphael 2008

Serves 4

1 eggplant sliced into rounds, ¾-inch thick, with the peel
3 tablespoon olive oil, plus more for the eggplant
2 onions, sliced
½ teaspoon turmeric
½ teaspoon curry powder
½ teaspoon red pepper flakes
2 fillets red snapper, cut into serving-sized pieces
5 tomatoes, peeled and sliced ⅓ inch thick

Sauce

Juice of 5 lemons
2 tablespoons tomato paste
½ teaspoon salt

Preheat oven to 450 degrees. Prepare a 12 x 9-inch baking pan with cooking spray.

Brush both sides of sliced eggplant with olive oil, place on a prepared cookie sheet and bake in a 450-degree oven until golden, about 10 minutes. Turn heat down to 400 degrees.

Heat olive oil in a sauté pan over medium-high heat and cook the onions with turmeric, curry and red pepper. Spread onion mixture in the prepared baking pan as a first layer. In the same sauté pan, sauté the fish until just seared and place over the onions. Place the prepared eggplant on top of the fish and the sliced tomatoes on the eggplant. Mix the lemon juice, tomato paste and salt in a small bowl and pour over the fish mixture. Bake in a 400 degree oven for 20 minutes.

This dish may be assembled ahead and refrigerated.

Tester's Comments: *Do not be put off by the amount of lemon juice called for in this dish. It helps marry the flavors of the tomatoes, eggplant, onions and spices.*

Trixie Putnam

Jane's Fish Stew

Martha Luemers' mother, Jane, found the origin of this recipe over 20 years ago in *Sunset* magazine, where it appeared as a microwave recipe for fish filets called "Red Snapper Vera Cruz." She has fiddled with the proportions and turned the fillets into bite-sized chunks to create the stew it is here. Adjust the amount of Tabasco to suit your palate, or even add a jalapeno or Serrano cut in half along with the tomatoes to flavor the broth. Remember to remove them before serving.

Martha Luemers
Robert 2008

Serves 4

4 tablespoons fresh lemon juice (1-2 lemons), divided
2 pounds red snapper fillets, pin bones removed
2 tablespoons butter
½ cup thinly sliced onion wedges
1 clove minced garlic
½ cup thinly sliced red or green pepper strips, or a combination of both
½ cup thinly sliced celery
1 (3- or 4-ounce) can or jar of mushrooms with juice
¼ cup dry white wine
1 can (14 ounces) diced tomatoes with juice
3 tablespoons prepared chili sauce
2 tablespoons capers
2 tablespoons chopped parsley
½ teaspoon dried thyme or 1 teaspoon fresh
Several dashes Tabasco sauce
¼ teaspoon salt or to taste

Unless your fish came off the boat the day you are cooking, wash in lemon water. Mix 2 tablespoons lemon juice with about a cup of cold water in a bowl and rinse the fish in the lemon water, then in plain water. Pat dry and cut into bite-sized chunks.

Melt butter over medium heat in a large sauté pan or heavy pot; cook onions and garlic until translucent, about 3 minutes. Add peppers, celery, mushrooms along with their juice, wine, canned tomatoes with their juice, chili sauce, capers, parsley, thyme, Tabasco and remaining lemon juice. Bring to a boil over high heat, then reduce the heat to low and simmer until celery and peppers are tender but still "al dente," about 10 minutes. Season to taste with salt. The stew can be made ahead to this point. Reheat to a simmer before starting.

Add fish chunks and simmer until fish is cooked, stirring only as needed to make sure all fish is submerged in liquid. If fish is at room temperature, this can take as little as 2 to 3 minutes. If fish is cold, it will take a few minutes longer.

Serve in bowls with crusty bread.

Chef's Note: The characteristic fishy smell that develops quickly as caught fish ages is the product of organic compounds that are not water-soluble. The addition of acid changes the compounds so that they become water soluble and can be washed away with water. Lemon is used as the acid in this recipe but vinegar would also work.

Testers Comments: For a more intense flavor and a thicker stew, after sautéing the onion and garlic, add the celery and continue cooking for 2 minutes. Then add the peppers and mushrooms (I used 1 cup fresh) and sauté 2 more minutes. Season this with ¼ teaspoon salt, thyme and an addition of ¼ teaspoon cumin and cook until fragrant, about 30 seconds. Turn the heat up to medium-high and add wine; cook until evaporated. Then add other ingredients as above.

Mary Pham

Seared Salmon with Greens
in a Ginger Vinaigrette

Marina Marcoux, a friend of Virginia Taylor's, was kind enough to give Virginia this recipe, which she cooks for her family at least once a month. It is easy to prepare, full of flavor and beautiful on the plate. The honey in the marinade creates a deep brown crust on the perfectly pink salmon.

Virginia Taylor
Geoff 2006
Anna 2007
Katie 2011

Serves 4

Salmon and Marinade

4 (5-ounce) salmon fillets
¼ cup soy sauce
2 tablespoons seasoned rice wine vinegar
1 tablespoon honey
1 teaspoon hot chili sauce (Sriracha Chili Sauce)
½ teaspoon ground coriander
½ teaspoon sesame oil
2 tablespoons peanut oil for searing the salmon

Ginger Vinaigrette

1 piece fresh ginger (1½ inches long) peeled and grated
1 clove garlic, minced
2 tablespoons seasoned rice wine vinegar
1 tablespoon soy sauce

1 tablespoon honey
½ teaspoon crushed red pepper
¼ cup peanut oil
½ teaspoon sesame oil

Salad

6 cups mixed greens
½ cup sliced almonds, toasted in oven at 350 degrees for 7 minutes

Place salmon fillets in a dish large enough to just hold them. Combine soy sauce, vinegar, honey, chili sauce, coriander and sesame oil in a small bowl and whisk. Pour sauce over salmon and marinate for at least 30 minutes (up to one hour) in the refrigerator. Remove from marinade and dry well.

For the vinaigrette, add the ginger, garlic, vinegar, soy sauce, honey, red pepper, peanut oil and sesame oil in a jar with a tight fitting lid or in a small bowl. Shake or whisk until emulsified. Set aside.

Place a sauté pan on medium-high heat and, when hot, add the peanut oil and then the salmon fillets. Sear on one side until well browned, about 3 minutes. Turn and sear on the other side until just pink in the middle, about 2 to 3 more minutes. While salmon is cooking, dress greens with some of the vinaigrette and toss in almonds. Place on large serving platter. When the salmon is done, place fillets on top of greens, pour a bit of the vinaigrette over the fish and serve immediately.

Sea Bass, Scallops and Clams in a Spicy Chili Broth

This one pot, quick and low-fat dish is a delicious marriage of its fresh ingredients. It is more brothy than a cioppino, with an additional kick from the Poblano chili and cilantro. This recipe came from a friend of the Kovachy's, who knew they liked soups—especially seafood chowders. We think he came up with a winner and Susan wanted to share it with you.

Susan Light
Tim Kovachy 2005
Benny Kovachy 2010

Serves 6

2 tablespoons canola oil
1 small onion, finely diced
2 large cloves garlic, minced
⅓ cup dry white wine
1 can (14.5 ounces) diced tomatoes with juice
2 cans (14 ounces) chicken broth
1 bay leaf
1 teaspoon fresh thyme
¼ cup fresh parsley, chopped
½ teaspoon pepper
1 can (6½ to 7 - ounces) chopped clams with liquid
½ Poblano or Anaheim chili, seeded and minced
1 pound sea bass or halibut, cut into 1- to 2-inch chunks
½ pound bay scallops
¼ cup fresh cilantro, chopped (optional)

Heat the oil in a large sauté pan over medium heat. Add onion and garlic and sauté until translucent. Add wine, bring to a boil and reduce about 1 minute.

146

Add tomatoes with their juice, chicken broth, bay leaf, thyme, parsley, and pepper to the pan. Drain the clams, reserving the clam liquid, and set aside. Add clam liquid to the pan. Bring to a boil; then reduce heat to low. Cover and simmer for 5 minutes. Add the minced chili and cook, covered for another 5 minutes. You can prepare the dish ahead of time up to this point; just remember to bring back to a simmer before you add the seafood.

Add the clams, sea bass and bay scallops to the tomato mixture and simmer 2 to 5 minutes, or just until fish and scallops turn opaque (cooking longer will make them dry and tough). Check a piece of fish after 2 minutes for doneness.

Ladle into bowls and top with cilantro if you wish.

Tester's Comments: *This recipe was not only easy, but my family also enjoyed the spicy after flavor. I used halibut to create my version, but any firm white fish would work. A side of sourdough or ciabatta bread for dipping in the delicious, light broth is an absolute must.*

Amy Magnuson

To create a deeper flavor in the broth and add to the finished look of the dish, I first seared the sea bass and scallops (I used the large, dry-packed sea scallops) in a hot sauté pan with a tablespoon of canola oil. I did this in two batches, first with the fish and next the scallops, setting them aside while I made the broth. I then used the same pan to sauté the onion and make the broth. I decreased the cooking time of the fish to two minutes, checking for doneness at one minute.

Virginia Taylor

147

Seared Yellow Fin Tuna
with Sun-Dried Tomato Vinaigrette

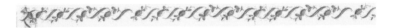

The combination of pale green leeks, yellow corn and green snow peas is magnificent against the seared tuna steak topped with the bright red tomato vinaigrette. While this dish is beautiful to look at, it is also a treat for the palate. Make sure you taste the vegetables, tuna and vinaigrette in one bite, for a true taste treat. Please note that the vinaigrette only gets better as it sits and develops flavor, so it is to your advantage to make it ahead of time. Serve this with Wheat Pilaf (page 253).

Felice Rebol
Jake Koval 2012

Serves 4

Sun-Dried Tomato Vinaigrette

½ cup balsamic vinegar
¾ cup sun-dried tomatoes, diced
¼ cup green onions, minced
1 clove garlic, minced
¾ cup extra-virgin olive oil (more or less depending on your taste)

Tuna and Vegetables

4 (6-ounce) Ahi or Yellow Fin tuna steaks
2 tablespoons crushed black peppercorns
3 tablespoons pure olive oil, divided
2 cups leeks, cut into julienne and blanched for one minute in boiling
   water

148

1 cup snow pea pods, cut into julienne and blanched for one minute in
    boiling water
1 cup white corn kernels
Salt and pepper to taste
1 tablespoon chives, or to taste, chopped (optional)

In a bowl, add the vinegar, sun-dried tomatoes, green onions and garlic.
Slowly whisk in ½ cup olive oil. Season to taste with salt and pepper and
add more olive oil if desired. Let sit at least two hours or overnight to
develop the flavors.

Brush about 1 tablespoon olive oil on the tuna steaks. Lightly coat with
the crushed pepper; season with salt. Heat 1 tablespoon olive oil in a sauté
pan over medium-high to high heat. Sear the tuna on both sides keeping it
medium rare, about 1 to 1½ minutes on each side.

In a separate sauté pan, heat the remaining 1 tablespoon olive oil over
medium heat and sauté the leeks, pea pods and corn until hot. Add seasoning
and chives.

Place the vegetable mixture on plate and spread evenly. Place the tuna on
top of the vegetables. Dress with vinaigrette just prior to serving.

Seared Sesame Seed Ahi Tuna with Sushi Rice

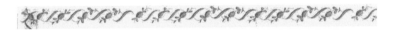

Slices of dark red tuna encrusted with sesame seeds and surrounded by salad greens and steamed squash creates a truly beautiful plate. The hardest part of preparing this dinner is the assembly. To serve this lovely meal while still hot, have a helper on hand to assist with the plating.

Cassie Maas
Kimberley Szabo 2009

Serves 6

Ahi Tuna

2 Ahi tuna steaks, 1 ½ inches thick, black portion removed
½ cup soy sauce, divided
1 tablespoon peanut oil
¼ cup black or white sesame seeds, or a combination of both
1 tablespoon prepared wasabi, or to taste

Sushi Rice

1½ cups short grain rice
½ teaspoon salt
Water for cooking
Soy sauce and rice wine vinegar to taste (optional)
1 sheet dried seaweed

Salad

6 cups salad greens
¼ cup mayonnaise
2 tablespoons ketchup
2 tablespoons seasoned rice wine vinegar or lemon juice
1 teaspoon sesame oil
2 crookneck squash, sliced in ½-inch pieces
2 patty pan squash, sliced in ½-inch pieces
2 teaspoons peanut oil
Salt to taste

Marinate Ahi steaks in ½ cup soy sauce for at least 30 minutes.

Place sesame seeds on a plate just large enough to hold a tuna steak. Remove the tuna from the soy sauce and shake dry then dip both sides in sesame seeds. Set aside in the refrigerator.

Mix remaining soy sauce and wasabi until combined.

Rinse the rice in water until water no longer turns white. Place in a medium-sized saucepan, covering the rice with water by about one knuckle worth or 1 inch. Add the salt and bring to a boil. Boil on medium-high heat, uncovered, until the water has absorbed and the rice is filled with craters. Lower heat to a simmer, cover and cook for 15 minutes. Let rest for at least 20 minutes without removing the lid.

For the dressing, whisk together mayonnaise, ketchup, vinegar or lemon juice and sesame oil. Set aside. Steam squash until tender but still crisp, about 4 minutes. Once cooked, toss with peanut oil and salt to taste. Set aside, cover to keep warm.

Heat a sauté pan large enough to fit both steaks over high heat. Once hot, quickly add oil then the tuna, and sear on one side for 1 minute. Turn and cook on the other side for an additional minute. Transfer to a plate and cover until ready to use.

(continued)

Assembly: Toss the greens lightly with the mayonnaise dressing (you may not need all of it). Place the salad on the serving plate with a few of the squash to the side. Fluff rice with a fork and add optional soy sauce and rice wine vinegar to taste if desired. Pack the rice into a small custard cup that has been lightly oiled. Unmold the rice onto the plate. Tear a piece of seaweed and place on top of rice. Cut the tuna steaks into ¼-inch slices and place decoratively on the rice. Top with a few teaspoons of the soy and wasabi mixture. Serve with additional soy and wasabi mixture.

Tester's Comments: *The trick to cooking good sushi rice is in the initial rinsing. Place the rice in a bowl and add the water. Mix with your fingers until the water becomes milky. Never let the rice set in the milky water. Drain the water and repeat until the water is clear. This will take about 5 minutes and the rice will become increasingly tender after each rinsing. Place the rice in your cooking pan and add the water. Let rest if possible, 30 minutes or up to 2 hours.*

Mary Pham

Poultry

Growing the Campus From Seed

The natural beauty of the Priory's campus is definitely beautiful but not at all natural! When the founding monks purchased the land that is now the campus, there were four oaks, an ash and a single palm tree. Every tree and shrub that now lends shade, form and beauty to our campus has been lovingly planted and nurtured.

In the early years, the Landscape Committee, a cadre of some of the most prominent ladies in the community (sometimes arriving in chauffer-driven cars), could be seen in their work clothes digging, planting and watering every week under the leadership of Mrs. Suzanne Eyre to make the school a garden spot. Father Egon recalls that the ladies fondly referred to Mrs. Eyre as Mother Superior or The General because of her organizational skills and attention to detail. The towering cedars that line the left side of the main driveway were three-feet tall when they were donated in the early 1960's. The redwoods on the right side of the driveway began life as seeds in containers that were tended by grounds manager Louis Kovacs and his colleague, Brother Francis. They raised 2,000 trees of six different species of conifer.

When a formal landscape master plan became necessary, Mrs. Eyre called her friend Thomas Church, one of the most influential American landscape architects of the 20th century. Credited as the father of what came to be known as the "California Style" of garden design, Church hesitated at first when Mrs. Eyre asked him to add the Priory to his firm's long list of clients. Undaunted, Mrs. Eyre prepared an elegant picnic. Under an umbrella against the backdrop of bare, dry earth, she served him pheasant and excellent French wine. He dictated on the spot all the elements of the master plan that became the lovely Priory campus that we enjoy today. At the top of the hill, the fountain that overlooks the campus is dedicated to Suzanne Eyre, and Church Square commemorates her friend's contribution to Woodside Priory's campus.

Pot Roasted Pheasant
in a Madeira Sauce

You can find pheasants at Andronico's or Draeger's, or you can special order them from your market. It is worth the effort to find these tasty birds and cook them up on your own. Pheasants can be known for being dry, but this oven-braised recipe creates a fork tender bird. Perfect for a fall dinner with mashed potatoes, polenta or Garlic Roasted Potatoes (page 271).

Mari-Lynne Earls
Jordan Amdahl 2006

Serves 6

2 pheasants, about 2 pounds each
2 tablespoons olive oil, plus some to prepare birds
Salt
Freshly ground pepper
8 ounces pancetta, diced
4 strips pancetta, left whole
4 ribs celery, coarsely chopped
3 sprigs fresh thyme
1½ cups Madeira wine, divided
1 cup chicken broth, avoid canned (frozen Perfect Additions is recommended)
5 tablespoons unsalted butter, sliced into ½-inch pieces and chilled

Preheat over to 450 degrees.

Rub pheasants with olive oil, salt and pepper. Set aside.

Heat 2 tablespoons olive oil in ovenproof heavy pot over low heat and sauté the diced pancetta. Remove pancetta from the pan and add pheasants, breast side down; sauté until lightly browned on each side. Situate the birds breast side up and add the pancetta to the pot, along with the celery, thyme and ½ cup wine. Bring to a boil. Place remaining slices of pancetta over pheasant breasts. Cover and place in the preheated oven. Roast for 30 minutes. Uncover and continue roasting until juices run clear, about 5 to 10 more minutes. Transfer pheasants to a warm platter, tent with foil and let rest while finishing sauce.

Remove thyme sprigs and pancetta strips from pot. Place casserole over high heat and add remaining wine and chicken broth. Simmer until reduced by at least half, swirl in the butter in pieces, strain if desired and spoon over the carved pheasants.

Tester's Notes: *We were so happy to have a new, unusual twist to our standard chicken recipe. The pheasant was tender, moist and not gamey, as we had feared. Just remember to reduce the sauce down until it has good flavor. It should just nap the birds.*

Emily Goldberg

Father Maurus's Fabulously Popular Auction Duck Dinner

From the day that the old farmhouse on the newly purchased Woodside Priory property was converted into a habitable condition, it served as the monastery, dormitory, dining hall, kitchen and recreation room. It is presumably in this kitchen that a monk, Father Leopold, the professor of Biology, began to cook. It was reasoned that a biology teacher might well differentiate from "what was poisonous and what was not." Father Maurus arrived at the Priory in 1963 and being the fine biologist that he is, he quickly followed in Father Leopold's footsteps. He perfected his dissecting technique of the poultry, in particular the duck, so that, by 1981, when the first auction was organized, Father Maurus' Hungarian Duck dinner became an item. From then on, the extremely popular duck dinners began being offered regularly. When asked how he prepares the duck, he states modestly that he would not dare call himself a cook, but the roasting of the duck he learned from his mother and has incorporated some of his own embellishments. What follows is, in narrative form, Father Maurus' duck recipe.

Father Maurus Nemeth

Serves 2

Begin with a good quality duck. "Good meat should speak for itself and the taste should be teased out," states Father Maurus.

Recall the anatomy of the duck before boning the whole bird. Split your bird in half and detach the meat from the ribs and carcass, which should leave you with two pieces, each with a de-boned breast and a leg. This portion constitutes a serving. Wash well in cold water. Salt each piece lightly and lay in the bottom of a roasting pan. Lightly season with white pepper and Hungarian paprika. This is the extent of the spices that are used.

Add:

2 stalks celery, chopped
1 onion, chopped
1 carrot, chopped
1 green pepper, chopped
2 bay leaves.

Preheat oven to 350 degrees.

Pour a cup of water in the bottom of the roasting pan with the ducks cover tightly with aluminum foil and simmer the duck halves in this manner for 1 hour and 15 minutes. Take off the aluminum cover and roast the duck for another 45 minutes until a lovely golden color has been achieved.

Father Maurus operates on the principle that poultry must be cooked thoroughly, and that this method of first braising the duck in moisture, then roasting to a golden brown insures that the meat is succulent and tender enough to fall easily from the fork when pierced. The fat in the meantime has been properly rendered and dripped off into the water.

The accompaniments are traditional as well. It is served with Wiener schnitzel, sweet and sour red cabbage, a special stuffing that has no recipe, stir-fry vegetable (some of the choices ones: snow peas and white asparagus, for example) and sweet potatoes. He always serves Cherries Jubilee for dessert.

This recipe serves 2. To produce the feast that Father Maurus offers at the auction, start with 12 whole ducks!

Cailles aux Raisins
(Squabs with Grapes)

It was Berkeley, 1975. Margaret Herzen was newly married, her husband was hungry and she had little cooking skills. Poor students that they were, the Herzens managed to scrape together some money for French cooking lessons. Here is a sample recipe from their endeavor. C'est bon et moins difficile, n'est ce pas? Encourage guest to use fingers when enjoying the delicate squab morsels. However, it would be gracious to provide finger bowls for each guest.

Margaret Herzen
Elena 2003
Juliana 2007

Serves 6

1½ cups seedless green grapes, removed from stem (cut grapes in ½ if they appear very large)
½ cup good quality cognac
6 (6-ounce) squabs, quails or game hens, reserving the livers (If using game hens, cut in half for the preparation and serving)

Pate

3 tablespoons unsalted butter, softened, divided
Salt and pepper
Pinch of ground thyme
1 tablespoon Madeira
6 slices day-old dense white bread, crusts removed
6 tablespoons butter, melted

For the Birds

4 tablespoons butter, clarified if possible
3 cups good quality, low-sodium chicken broth
¼ – ½ teaspoon ground thyme
1 bay leaf, crushed
1 clove garlic, minced
1 large shallot, diced
¼ teaspoon white pepper
1 tablespoon arrowroot blended with 1 tablespoon of water
2 tablespoons unsalted butter

Preheat oven to 350 degrees.

Marinate grapes in the cognac at room temperature for at least 1 hour, stirring occasionally.

Sauté livers (chicken livers maybe substituted if using quails or no livers are included) in 1 tablespoon of butter over medium-high heat. Season with salt, pepper and pinch or two of thyme. Mash the sautéed livers with a fork. Turn off heat, add 2 tablespoons of softened butter and Madeira. Reserve in a small bowl.

Place the 6 slices of bread on baking sheet and brush them evenly with the melted butter. Toast in oven until golden, about 7 to 10 minutes.

Preheat over to 450 degrees.

Truss the birds with string. In a 12-inch skillet, heat 4 tablespoons butter over medium-high heat. Season the birds with salt and pepper and, when butter begins to sizzle, brown the birds (turning with tongs) until they are richly and evenly colored. Place the skillet on the middle shelf of the oven and roast for 8 to 10 minutes for the squab and quail; at least 20 minutes for the game hens. To test for doneness, prick the thigh of a squab with the point of a small knife; the juices should run pale and pink (clear for the quail and game hen).

(continued)

163

If the squab juices are still red, roast the birds for 2 or 3 minutes longer. Squabs are traditionally cooked to medium rare, while the game hens and quail to medium. Transfer to a platter and let rest, tented with foil while preparing the sauce.

Drain the grapes in a sieve over a bowl, reserving cognac marinate, and put them aside. Pour off the fat from the skillet and add the reserved marinade. Boil over high heat, stirring constantly and scraping in the browned particles that cling to the bottom and sides of the pan, until reduced by half. Add chicken broth, thyme, crushed bay leaf, garlic, shallot and pepper. Continue cooking until reduced by half again.

Stirring with a wire whisk, gradually add the arrowroot mixture to the reduced stock. Continue to cook, stirring constantly for 3 to 4 minutes, until the sauce is smooth and has thickened. Be sure to reduce the 3 cups of liquid chicken broth to ½ the volume, otherwise the one tablespoon of the arrowroot will not thicken the sauce to the proper consistency. The sauce will should run thin, look glossy and have a lovely cognac fragrance. Strain and taste for seasoning. Swirl in 2 tablespoons of unsalted butter. Mix in ²/₃ of the grapes, reserving the rest for decoration.

Presentation: Spread the liver pâté on the toasted bread slices, dividing evenly among the six slices. Arrange the canapés on a platter. Place the bird over each canapé and spoon some sauce with the grapes over it. Decorate the platter with the remaining grapes.

Pesto Chicken Rolls

The perfect marriage between the mild taste of chicken and the flavorful bite of basil pesto, this entrée is ideal served on a bed of farm fresh chopped tomatoes just heated through in tasty extra-virgin olive oil, with a dash of salt and balsamic vinegar. Add steamed cauliflower and broccoli for a low carbohydrate meal or serve as suggested with pasta.

Lisa Plain
Hap 2006
Alex 2008

Serves 4

2 whole boneless chicken breasts, halved, cartilage and skin removed
Salt to taste
16 tablespoons pesto, divided, homemade or purchased
4 tablespoons grated Parmesan cheese plus additional for sprinkling

Preheat oven to 350 degrees.

Pound chicken breasts between 2 sheets waxed paper until about ¼-inch thick and sprinkle each side with salt. Spread 2 tablespoons pesto on each breast, then top with 1 tablespoon grated Parmesan, covering the entire pounded breast. Roll breasts starting on a more narrow end and place seam side down in an ungreased baking dish. Spread 2 teaspoons of pesto on each roll, and sprinkle with additional Parmesan cheese.

Bake for 30 minutes. Let rest, covered, for five minutes. To serve, cut each roll in half at an angle like an egg roll, laying one flat and balancing the cut side up against the flat roll. Serve with pasta, buttered, or in a light tomato sauce.

165

Beer Can Chicken

Adapted from *Weber's Big Book of Grilling* by Jamie Purviance, this recipe steam roasts the chicken to perfection as it balances on a half-filled can of beer. If you plan on leaving the bird unattended, set it on an aluminum pie plate to protect the meat from the flare-ups that can happen even on indirect heat.

The Corkery Family
Kelsey 2007
Teagan 2009

Serves 4 to 6

2 teaspoons dry mustard
2 teaspoons granulated onion
2 teaspoons paprika (preferably Mexican paprika)
2 teaspoons kosher salt
1 teaspoon granulated garlic
1 teaspoon ground coriander
1 teaspoon cumin
1 teaspoon black pepper
1 whole chicken, 4 to 5 pounds
3 teaspoons vegetable oil
1 (12 ounce can) beer

Prepare and heat barbecue grill to medium heat.

Combine mustard, granulated onion, paprika, salt, granulated garlic, coriander, cumin and black pepper in a small bowl.
Remove and discard the neck, giblets and any excess fat from the chicken.
Rinse the chicken inside and out under cold water and pat dry well with a

towel. Brush the chicken all over with the vegetable oil, then rub with the dry ingredients to completely cover the outside of the chicken.

Take the open beer can (with two gulps of beer removed, to slightly lower the liquid level) and set on a flat surface. Slide the chicken over the top of the beer can, fitting the upright can snugly inside the cavity. The legs should be touching the surface of the counter to help balance the chicken. Transfer the bird to the heated grill, keeping the can upright. (The bird will be balanced on the can, stabilized with its two legs on the grill.)

Grill, covered, over indirect medium heat until the juices run clear and the internal temperature reaches 170 degrees in the breast and 180 degrees in the thickest part of the thigh; approximately 1 to 1½ hours.

Wearing barbecue mitts or clean kitchen gloves, carefully remove the chicken and the can from the grill, being careful not to spill the beer. (It will be hot!) Let the chicken rest for about 10 minutes before lifting it from the can. Discard the beer. Cut the chicken into serving pieces. Serve warm.

Tester's Comments: *I used a whole fresh lemon instead of the oil to first rub on the bird, then rubbed the entire bird, including inside the cavity and under the skin, with the seasoning spices. No extra calories and even more flavor.*

Mary Pham

Chicken Marbella

Originally from Julee Rosso and Sheila Lukins' *The Silver Palate Cookbook*, this recipe was given to us by two different families as their favorite! Our tester gave it a big thumbs up and, with a fifteen minute prep time, it is a definite winner! The combination of prunes, green olives and capers—or sweet, salty and sour—makes a plain roasted chicken divine! You must cook up a side of rice to sop up the juices.

Sharon Traeger
Alix 2011

Roberta Harryman
William 2007
Ryan 2009

Serves 16

4 chickens, 2 ½ pounds each, quartered
1 head of garlic, peeled and finely puréed in a food processor
¼ cup dried oregano
2 teaspoons kosher salt
1 teaspoon freshly ground black pepper
½ cup red wine vinegar
½ cup olive oil
1 cup pitted prunes
½ cup pitted Spanish green olives
½ cup capers with a bit of juice
6 bay leaves
1 cup brown sugar
1 cup white wine
¼ cup Italian parsley or fresh cilantro, finely chopped

168

In a large bowl combine garlic, oregano, salt, pepper, vinegar, olive oil, prunes, olives, capers with juice, and bay leaves. Add chicken, cover and marinate, refrigerated, overnight. Can also be placed in an extra-large ziplock bag.

Preheat oven to 350 degrees.

Arrange chicken in a single layer in one or two large, shallow baking pans and spoon marinade evenly over chickens. Sprinkle chicken pieces with brown sugar and pour white wine around them.

Bake for 50 minutes to 1 hour, basting frequently with pan juices. Chicken is done when thigh pieces, pricked with a fork at their thickest point, yield clear yellow (rather than pink) juice.

Using a slotted spoon transfer chicken, prunes, olives and capers to a serving platter. Moisten with a few spoonfuls of pan juices and sprinkle generously with parsley or cilantro. Pass remaining pan juices in a sauceboat.

To serve Chicken Marbella cold, cool to room temperature in cooking juices before transferring to a serving platter. If chicken has been covered and refrigerated, return to room temperature before serving. Spoon some of the reserved juices over chicken.

Sautéed Chicken Breasts with Fresh Orange Salsa

Here is a fast and easy way to brighten up the flavor of plain sautéed chicken breasts. This is a versatile salsa—it can also be served on fish—allowing you to be creative. You can adjust the heat of the salsa by reducing or increasing the amount of jalapeños. Irina Sarkisov even likes to substitute a mango for one of the oranges

Irina Sarkisov
Katya 2006

Serves 4

Salsa

3 Valencia oranges, peel and white pith removed with a sharp knife
¾ cup chopped radishes
¼ cup chopped green olives
3 tablespoons finely chopped fresh cilantro
2 tablespoons minced red onion
2 tablespoons minced jalapeño pepper, or to taste

Chicken

2 tablespoons flour
2 teaspoons ground cumin
¼ teaspoon salt
⅛ teaspoon freshly ground pepper
4 boneless, skinless chicken breast halves (about 5 ounces each)
2 teaspoons oil

Holding the peeled oranges over a bowl, remove the individual orange sections by cutting between the membranes to release sections into the bowl. Squeeze the remaining juice from the membranes into the bowl. Stir in the radishes, olives, cilantro, red onion and jalapeño pepper.

Mix flour, cumin, salt and pepper in a large plastic food bag. Add chicken, close bag and shake until evenly coated. Heat oil in a large nonstick skillet over medium heat. Add chicken and cook, turning once, 6 to 7 minutes, until golden outside and juices run clear when meat is pierced. Transfer to a serving platter, spoon on salsa and serve.

Serve with sautéed or steamed spinach.

Tester's Comments: *This is a very straightforward recipe that my family loved. I would recommend letting the salsa sit for a half an hour at room temperature to allow the flavors to develop.*

Tamra Tehaney

Chicken Breasts
with Asparagus and Carrots

Taken from *The 60 Minute Gourmet* by Pierre Franey, this is a Traeger family favorite, and will soon be one of yours. It is an elegant and colorful dish with the vegetables and sauce complementing the subtle chicken. All you need to make this dish a complete meal is a side of rice, or pasta.

Sharon Traeger
Alix 2011

Serves 4

Salt to taste
8 fresh large asparagus spears, trimmed and peeled
1 carrot, julienned in 2-inch lengths
2 whole boneless and skinless chicken breasts, cut in half
Freshly ground pepper to taste
1 to 2 tablespoons flour
3 tablespoons butter, divided
1 tablespoon shallots, finely chopped
½ cup dry white wine
1 tablespoon tomato paste
¼ cup fresh or canned chicken broth
2 tablespoons heavy cream

Bring about 4 cups water to a boil in a medium saucepan with enough salt to taste like seawater.

Fill a medium-sized bowl with ice and fill with water. Drop the vegetables into the boiling water and cook about 4 minutes or until tender-crisp. Do not overcook. Drain well and place in ice bath to stop the cooking process. Drain, dry and set aside.

Sprinkle the four chicken pieces with salt and pepper to taste. Dredge lightly in flour and shake off excess.

Heat 2 tablespoons of the butter in a skillet over medium-high heat. Before the butter browns, add the chicken pieces. Cook on one side about 4 minutes. Turn and cook on the other side until golden brown, about 2 to 4 minutes. Cover, lower the heat to medium-low and cook an additional 3 to 5 minutes until cooked through but still tender.

Transfer the chicken to a warm platter and cover with aluminum foil. To the same skillet, over medium heat, add the shallots. Stir and cook briefly. Add the wine and cook until reduced by half over medium-high heat. A lower heat may be used, it will just take longer. Add the tomato paste, stir, and then add the chicken broth stirring well to incorporate the tomato paste. Stir in the cream and continue cooking a few more minutes, until it has a sauce consistency.

While the sauce is reducing, heat the remaining tablespoon of butter in a skillet over medium heat. Add the asparagus and carrots, salt and pepper to taste. Cook just to heat through and coated with butter. The vegetables can also be placed in a microwave proof dish with the butter, melted, seasoned with salt and pepper then reheated in the microwave until hot, about 2 minutes.

Arrange equal portions of asparagus and carrots between the chicken breast pieces. Spoon the sauce over the chicken and serve.

Tester's Comments: *I made this recipe for a dinner party and everyone thought it was a keeper. My only recommendation would be to pound or butterfly the breast for quicker cooking. If you do this, I would sauté the pounded breast until brown, about 2 to 3 minutes, turn over and continue browning until just cooked, about another 2 minutes depending on how thin the cutlets are. Set the cooked breasts aside and then start with the sauce. You can even reheat the breasts in the warm sauce.*

Trixie Putman

Turkey Picatta

This is one of Virginia Taylor's staple recipes for her family meals. She loves it with turkey tenderloins because they are easy to prepare, but this recipe could also be done with the traditional veal or chicken breasts sliced in half and pounded thin. Katie Taylor thinks this recipe is wonderful with either Pesto Pasta or Curried Orzo Pasta with Almonds and Currants (page 238).

Virginia Taylor
Geoff 2006
Anna 2007
Katie 2011

Serves 6

2 turkey tenderloins, thinly sliced on an angle and pounded to an even ¼-inch width
Salt and pepper to taste
Flour for dredging
2 to 4 tablespoons olive oil for frying
2 shallots, minced
½ cup dry white wine
2 cups chicken stock
1 tablespoon lemon juice, or to taste
3 tablespoons capers, drained
Lemon slices

Salt and pepper turkey scaloppini. Place a mound of flour on a plate for dredging the scaloppini. Heat a large sauté pan over high heat and add olive oil to just cover the bottom of your pan. Dredge enough scaloppinis to fit into the pan in the flour, shaking off excess, and place in the almost smoking oil. Do not dredge all the meat before, or the flour will become moist and gummy. Turn heat down to medium-high and cook for 2 to 3 minutes on one side, until browned and almost cooked. Turn over and cook for 30 seconds until just done. (Cook well on one side and kiss the other side with the heat, that is it.) Remove to a plate and continue with the remaining fillets, adding more oil as needed. Set all the turkey aside as you make the sauce.

Turn the heat down to medium-low and add a bit more oil if needed; sauté shallots until browned, scraping up the browned bits of flour which will thicken and flavor your sauce. Add the wine and reduce by half. Add the chicken stock and reduce again, by half over medium heat. Season with salt and lemon juice. The sauce will not be thick at this point but should have flavor.

Return the scaloppini into the sauce, swirling each scaloppini in the sauce. The flour on the cutlets will thicken the sauce. Continue with each cutlet and heat until sauce is bubbling and turkey is hot. Top with capers and lemon slices if you desire.

Tester's Comments: *My children, who thought they did not like turkey tenders, loved this dish. For even easier preparation, I will use chicken tenders which I will use whole, pounding them down to make an even thickness.*

Sharon Traeger

Chicken with Currants

The influence of crème de cassis and currants in the sauce creates this rich and flavorful chicken dish. Originally, this recipe was from *Sunset* magazine, but Charlie Lombard has cooked it so many times that he has adapted this version as his own. We think it's a winner—especially served with Fragrant Barley Casserole (page 254) or Wheat Pilaf (page 253).

Charlie Lombard
Austin 2009

Serves 4

4 chicken legs with thighs
Salt
White pepper
Nutmeg
2 tablespoons olive oil
2 cloves garlic, minced
2 tablespoons fruit vinegar (blackberry, raspberry or your choice)
2 tablespoons tomato paste
¾ cup chicken broth
¼ cup white wine
¼ cup crème de cassis
½ cup currants

2 tablespoons flour
2 tablespoons softened butter

Dust chicken with salt, pepper and nutmeg.

Add oil and chicken to a sauté pan and over medium heat fry the chicken

176

until brown, about 6 minutes per side. Turn heat down to medium and add garlic, vinegar and tomato paste; cook for about 30 seconds.

Add broth, wine, crème de cassis and currants to the sauté pan and bring to a boil. Cover, turn heat down to low and cook for 25 minutes or until chicken is done.

Mix the flour and softened butter in a small bowl until you have a soft paste. Remove chicken from pan, bring sauce to a boil and add the roux in bits until it has dissolved into the sauce, stirring constantly. A whisk works well here. Cook over medium-high heat until pan drippings have thickened to a sauce consistency. Place the chicken along with its juices back into the sauce to reheat slightly.

Serve chicken over rice, covered with the sauce and some freshly cooked green beans with garlic and rosemary. To make a perfect meal open a bottle of Pinot Noir.

Chicken and Artichoke Stroganoff

Buy chicken tenders or cut up boneless, skinless breasts to make this easy, flavorful dish even quicker. It's great served over fettuccine noodles with a side of toasty garlic bread and a big, mixed green salad.

Kelly Pettit
Angela 2008

Serves 6

2 tablespoons flour
½ teaspoon dried mustard
½ teaspoon dried dill weed
1 (6-ounce) jar marinated artichoke hearts, sliced into bite-sized pieces, saving the marinade
½ cup chopped onion
1 clove garlic, minced
2 whole boneless breasts of chicken, split, skinned and cut into strips
¾ cup water
2 chicken bouillon cubes
½ cup sour cream
Hot, cooked pasta of your choice

In a small bowl, mix flour, mustard and dill weed with the drained marinade from the artichokes (save 2 tablespoons to cook the chicken) and set aside.

Spoon the 2 remaining tablespoons of marinade oil into a skillet and heat. When just shimmering, add onion and garlic; sauté until soft. Add chicken and continue cooking over moderate heat for 5 minutes, or just until chicken is lightly browned but still not fully cooked. Add water and bouillon cubes;

let cubes melt into the water.

Once the bouillon cubes have dissolved, stir mustard/flour mixture into pan liquid. Bring to a boil, stirring constantly. Reduce heat and simmer 2 to 3 minutes, or until chicken is cooked through and sauce has thickened slightly. Stir in sour cream, mixing until smooth and the sauce is hot, but be careful not to let it boil. Add artichoke hearts and serve over pasta.

Tester's Comments: *Our family thoroughly enjoyed this dish. The artichoke hearts give this dish added texture and blend nicely with the creamy dill sauce. I left this dish in a warming oven for several hours without losing any flavor.*

Sharon Traeger

Tandoori Butter Chicken
with Raita

A Northern Indian classic, this recipe has been perfected over the years by Emmeline Hazaray, a friend of the Purvin's from India. The spiciness of the chilies is tempered by the cool crunch of the Raita. If you have never tried cooking Indian food, this is the recipe to get you started.

Francesca Purvin
Colton 2011

Serves 6

2 tablespoons olive oil

1 onion, minced

¼ teaspoon cinnamon

1 inch piece of piece ginger, peeled and sliced

3 cloves garlic, skinned

1 to 2 Serrano chilies or to taste, roughly chopped

½ cup chopped cilantro leaves with stems

2 pounds skinless, boneless chicken thighs or breasts cut into 1-inch pieces

10 blanched almonds and 10 whole raw cashews, finely ground in a food processor

1½ cups peeled, seeded and chopped tomatoes

2 tablespoons tomato paste

1 teaspoon Kissan Tandoori powder (available in any Indian grocery store or the international section of your market)

1 teaspoon salt, or to taste

½ to ¾ cup sour cream

Cilantro leaves for garnish, chopped

½ cup sliced almonds, toasted for 7 minutes in a 350 degree oven

Chicken

Heat oil is a large sauté pan over medium heat. Add onion and cinnamon and fry until the onions are lightly browned.

While the onions are cooking, place the ginger, garlic, cilantro and Serrano chilies in a food processor and pulse until completely minced and smooth. Add to the onions, along with 2 tablespoons of water, and cook until the mixture is dry, about 2 minutes.

Add the chicken pieces and sauté until the chicken has turned white. Pour in the ground nuts, chopped tomatoes with juice, tomato paste and Tandoori powder; mix thoroughly. Bring to a simmer, cover, reduce heat to low and cook for 20 minutes.

Add sour cream to taste, mix and simmer, uncovered, for an additional 10 minutes on low heat. Salt to taste.

Garnish with cilantro leaves and toasted almonds, serve with raita (recipe below) and Basmati rice.

Raita

1 small sweet yellow onion, chopped in ¼-inch cubes
2 small tomatoes, cut in half, seeded and chopped in ¼-inch cubes
3 inches of cucumber, seeded and chopped in ¼-inch cubes
½ cup lightly chopped cilantro
½ teaspoon salt, or to taste
1 teaspoon sugar
Freshly ground black pepper to taste
½ cup plain whole-fat yogurt

Mix the onion, tomatoes, cucumber and cilantro in a medium-sized bowl; season with salt and pepper. Add the yogurt and mix well. Let sit for at least 15 minutes but no more than two hours before serving.

Tempting Thai Chicken
with Spicy Peanut Sauce

Alix Traeger (Class of 2011) considers this recipe, from *Desperation Dinners* by Beverly Mills and Alicia Ross, her absolute favorite. It's quick, simple and full of Asian-inspired flavor. To give this dish more punch, use spicy chili sauce instead of the cayenne pepper called for in the Peanut Sauce. You can also stir-fry a handful of snow peas with the chicken to add some crunch. Once you try this recipe it will become one of your family standards.

Sharon Traeger
Alix 2011

Serves 4

Spicy Peanut Sauce

1½ tablespoons creamy peanut butter
2 tablespoons vegetable oil
2 tablespoons reduced-sodium soy sauce
2 tablespoons sugar
2 teaspoons seasoned rice wine vinegar
½ teaspoon dark sesame oil
⅛ teaspoon ground cayenne pepper (optional)

Chicken

4 skinless, boneless chicken breast halves, sliced into short strips about ½ inch wide
2 teaspoons vegetable oil
1 tablespoon minced garlic

182

1 tablespoon chopped ginger
¾ cup scallions in ¼-inch slices (both green and white)
1 can (8 ounces) sliced bamboo shoots, drained and dried
⅓ cup dry roasted peanuts, chopped
1 tablespoon reduced-sodium soy sauce
1 tablespoon dry sherry
1 teaspoon sugar

Combine the peanut butter, oil, soy sauce, sugar, vinegar, sesame oil and pepper in a small bowl and whisk until well combined. Set aside.

Heat the oil in a 12-inch nonstick skillet over high heat. Season the chicken lightly with salt. Add to the hot skillet and stir-fry for one minute. Add the garlic and ginger; continue cooking until the chicken is no longer pink, about 5 to 7 minutes.

Add the scallions, bamboo shoots, peanuts, soy sauce, sherry and sugar. Stir well, then add the peanut sauce and stir well again. Cook until heated through, about 2 minutes. Serve over a bed of steamed rice.

Tester's Comments: *This recipe is adaptable; many substitutions are possible. Try water chestnuts for the bamboo shoots, chunky peanut butter for creamy, white wine for the sherry or hot water for the oil in the sauce. I added a squeeze of fresh lime at the end and loved the results. A great, fun weeknight dish!*

Lila Fitzgerald

Stir-fried Chicken with Mango

This recipe resulted from a combined effort between the recipe originator, Ingrid Lai, and the tester, Keith Low, who is the Chinese chef in his family. The original recipe was created for the microwave and since our tester was not familiar with this type of cooking, Keith adapted it for a traditional wok. The results were stunning, better than a restaurant's version in all of our opinions. Use a firm mango for best results. You may also substitute shrimp for the chicken.

Ingrid Lai
Anthony Shu 2012

Serves 4

Sauce

2 teaspoons white vinegar
½ tablespoon tomato paste
1½ teaspoons sugar
3 tablespoons water
1 tablespoon soy sauce

Chicken Marinade

8 ounces chicken breasts cut in strips
2 teaspoons canola oil
2 teaspoons light soy sauce
1 teaspoon cornstarch
A few drops of sesame oil
Black pepper to taste

Stir-Fry

2 tablespoons canola oil
5 thin slices of peeled ginger
½ green bell pepper cut in thin strips
½ red bell pepper cut into thin strips
1 mango, peeled and julienned

Combine the vinegar, tomato paste, sugar, water and soy sauce in a small bowl; set aside.

Combine the oil, soy sauce, cornstarch, sesame oil and pepper, mixing well. Evenly coat the chicken and marinate for 30 minutes at room temperature.

Heat a well seasoned wok or nonstick pan on medium-high heat until hot. Add the two tablespoons of oil to the pan, when shimmering, add ginger slices and stir-fry 15 to 20 seconds. Add chicken, spreading them in the wok. Cook, undisturbed, 1 to 2 minutes, letting chicken begin to brown. Stir-fry another 1 to 2 minutes until chicken is barely cooked through. Transfer chicken to a plate and set aside.

Add red and green bell peppers and stir-fry 1 to 2 minutes, then add green onions. Stir-fry an additional 1 minute or until the peppers are cooked to your liking. Transfer peppers and onions to the plate with the chicken.

In the hot wok, slowly pour in the sauce, as it will splatter. Cook for 20 seconds. Return chicken and peppers to the wok and stir-fry for 30 seconds to heat. Add mango and heat through, about 10 to 15 seconds.

Garnish with cilantro sprigs and serve immediately over steamed rice.

Auntie Helen's Chicken Curry Casserole

Here is our offering of a classic casserole dish that has been served for years at all large Landers family gatherings. No "official" recipe exits. The casserole just comes from Roberta's memory of making it with her aunt year after year. We think we've finally created the official recipe for you to share at your next family potluck.

Roberta Landers
Hilary 2007
Rachael 2011

Serves 10 to 12

5 boneless chicken breasts poached and chopped (or 5 cups leftover chicken)
2 cups sliced celery
2 minced green onions, both green and white parts
2 cans cream of chicken soup (not low-fat or low-sodium)
1 tablespoon fresh lemon juice
1 cup mayonnaise
½ cup water
1 tablespoon curry powder, or to taste
1 cup sliced almonds, divided
3 cups cooked basmati rice
2 cups broccoli heads, blanched until tender-crisp
1½ cups Cheddar cheese, divided
1 teaspoon salt

Preheat oven to 350 degrees.

Mix chicken, celery, green onions, soup, lemon juice, mayonnaise, water and curry together in a bowl. In a large bowl, mix rice, ⅓ cup of almonds,

186

broccoli, 1 cup of cheese and salt. Add chicken mixture and mix well. Pour into a casserole and bake for about 30 minutes. Top with remaining cheese and ⅔ cup almonds and bake uncovered for another 15 minutes until the cheese is melted and almonds are crisp.

Chicken Patties
with Fresh Herbs

For a unique, new twist to chicken or turkey, these patties are easy to make and full of fresh herb flavor. Mary Pham has provided the three different herb combinations that are her family's favorites, but be creative and discover your own favorite combinations of flavor! Serve with Fragrant Barley Casserole (page 254) or Garlic Roasted Potatoes (page 271) and wilted greens of your choice.

Mary Pham
David Low 2010

Serves 4

1½ pounds ground chicken or turkey
3 large eggs
2 tablespoons olive oil
Salt and pepper to taste
½ cup of any combination of fresh herbs (see below), chopped
4 cloves garlic, finely minced, or to taste
3 shallots, finely minced
Chicken broth or water to deglaze the pan

Optional herbs: Fresh thyme, sage (not more than 5 leaves), pineapple sage, parsley, chives, oregano, mint (not more than 10 leaves), sorrel, tarragon, cilantro, rosemary (not more than ½ sprig) and lemon zest

Mary's family's favorite herb mixes:
    Spring/early summer: thyme, parsley, sage
    Summer: sorrel, parsley, pineapple sage
    Winter: parsley, thyme and lemon zest
    Anytime of year: cilantro, parsley and mint

Mix ground meat, eggs, salt, pepper and herbs in a large bowl.

In a large nonstick skillet over medium-high heat, heat olive oil until hot but not smoking, and add the chicken mixture, spreading it to fill the pan. Cook for 10 minutes, or until brown. You can also make individual patties (four to six) but be careful not to overcook the meat.

Flip chicken patty by dividing it into quarters, then flipping each quarter over individually. Cook for 5 to 6 minutes more; the patty should be soft and moist but also fully cooked. If overcooked, it will harden.

Remove patty to serving platter. Keep warm. Deglaze pan with chicken broth or water and pour over patty.

Tester's Comments: *Our family found this adaptable recipe fresh tasting with an addition of lemon zest. The patty's loose texture could be made firmer with the addition of ½ cup of dried, plain breadcrumbs.*

Lila Fitzgerald

Picadillo

Unusual flavor combinations liven up ground turkey in this family friendly meal from *Cooking Light* magazine. While the raisins, olives and capers create an exotic flavor, if you want to add some punch, try sautéing a Serrano chili in with the onion.

Betsy Haehl
Alicia Kriewall 2007

Serves 4

1 teaspoon olive oil
1 cup finely chopped onion
1 teaspoon salt, or to taste
1 pound ground turkey
3 garlic cloves, minced
1 cup low-sodium chicken broth
⅓ cup raisins
⅓ cup coarsely chopped pimiento-stuffed olives
3 tablespoons capers
1 tablespoon tomato paste
¼ teaspoon freshly ground black pepper
3 cups hot cooked rice
Parsley sprigs (optional)

Heat oil in a large nonstick skillet over medium-high heat. Add onion and salt to taste and sauté for 5 minutes. Add turkey and garlic stirring to crumble, and cook for 5 minutes, or until browned. Add broth, raisins, olives, capers, tomato paste and pepper; stir well. Bring to a boil. Cover, reduce heat and simmer for 25 minutes.

Serve with rice. Garnish with parsley sprigs, if desired.

Beef, Pork and Lamb

Father Martin's Crosiers

Many of us in the Priory community have admired the tall clocks that Father Martin builds every year for the annual auction, and we have all sat in the beautiful pews he has made for the chapel. Few of us, however, have had the privilege of seeing any of the crosiers that Father Martin has been called to make for bishops across the nation. A crosier is the stylized shepherd's crook carried by a bishop and used at many of the liturgical functions over which he officiates. Use of the crosier is mentioned in church documents as far back as the fifth century, and symbolizes the bishop leading his community as a shepherd leads his flock.

The most recent "Crosier by Martin" was commissioned by Bishop Wang of San Francisco. Father Martin formed the gracefully curved crook of black walnut and Brazilian rosewood and made transitional pieces of ebony; the staff is a beautiful length of cherry wood. Four pieces of jade, set in silver by Priory art teacher Reed Easley and representing the four Gospels, are inlaid in the node. Each variety of wood is inherently beautiful, but the use of the various woods also symbolizes the universality and diversity of the Church. The black walnut is from the southern states; the cherry is from the east coast; ebony is from Africa; rosewood is from South America; and jade is especially prized in Asia.

Father Martin's crosiers can come apart for convenience in travel, and finding an appropriate carrying case is as big a challenge as making the staff. Bishop Wang's carrying case is light and sturdy; it was a case for a pool cue before being converted by Father Martin to protect the bishop's staff.

A photograph of Bishop Wang's crosier appears on the inside flap of the back cover of the cookbook.

Beef Stroganoff

20 years ago, a friend who loves to cook gave this recipe to Marjorie Brent, and it is still fresh today. The beauty of this recipe is it can be made in advance and popped into the oven at dinner time. Like any good stew, this dish is better the next day so make extras. If you do double the recipe, cook your meat in batches to ensure searing your meat instead of steaming your meat.

Marjorie Brent
Laura 2004
Ian 2007

Serves 4

3 tablespoons butter, divided
1 onion, sliced
½ pound mushrooms, sliced
1 pound stroganoff (top sirloin cut into thin strips)
2 tablespoons flour
2 cubes bouillon in 1 cup hot water
1 tablespoon Dijon mustard
1 tablespoon Worcestershire sauce
1 tablespoon ketchup
½ cup sour cream

Melt 2 tablespoons butter in a large skillet over medium-low heat; sauté onions until translucent, approximately 10 minutes. Remove and place in a 2 ½-quart casserole; add mushrooms to skillet and sauté until soft, approximately 5 minutes and add to casserole. Brown beef in skillet, adding more butter if necessary and add to casserole.

Melt remaining tablespoon of butter in skillet and add flour; mix well and cook for 1 minute. Stir in bouillon then add mustard, Worcestershire and ketchup. Cook for 3 minutes until well combined—using a whisk works well to incorporate ingredients. Cool mixture for 10 minutes and then add sour cream. Add to the casserole with the mushrooms, onions and beef and mix well.

Bake for 45 minutes. Serve over rice or noodles

Tester's Comments: *Yummy! I am going to have to retire my much more elaborate recipe for stroganoff in favor of this one!*

Patty Turnquist

Blue Cheese Tenderloin Steaks

There's nothing like the combination of delicate beef tenderloin and the rich, tangy flavor of a strong blue cheese. This is an ideal recipe to use if you want to spice up a steak dinner without too much prep work: it's fast and straightforward. This meal is great in the summer served with seasonal grilled vegetables or in the winter with a hearty side of Garlic Roasted Potatoes (page 271).

Pamela Martinson
Marisa 2010

Serves 4

2 tablespoons cream cheese, softened
4 tablespoons crumbled blue cheese
2 tablespoons butter
2 teaspoons finely minced onion
Salt and pepper to taste
4 beef tenderloin steaks, cut 1- to 1½-inches thick
1 clove garlic, halved
2 teaspoons chopped parsley

Preheat broiler.

Combine cream cheese, blue cheese, butter and onion; season with salt and pepper to taste and set aside.

Rub steaks with cut surface of garlic. Place steaks on rack in broiler pan so the surface of the meat is 2 to 3 inches from the heat.

Cook for 5 minutes on one side; season well with salt. Turn and cook for 3 additional minutes.

Top each steak with an equal amount of the cheese mixture. Broil 1 minute longer. Remove from oven and garnish with chopped parsley. Let rest, lightly covered, for 5 minutes before serving.

Tester's Comments: *The silence followed by humming around the dinner table indicated this dish was a big winner! We all loved this one.*

Marjorie Brent

Roasted Whole Filet Mignon with a Port Wine Sauce

It is a tradition for the parents of the graduating class of 2011 to get together while the kids are dancing away at school events. Virginia Taylor has made this filet a number of times for their party because it is simple to prepare, is easily transported for pot lucks, feeds a crowd and is loved by the masses. The filet is wonderful on it's own but the port wine sauce brings this dish to the realm of Nirvana. Serve with the Provençal Au Gratin Potatoes (page 270) and some wilted spinach for a dinner party menu your guests will never forget.

Chef's Note: The key to this roast is to properly prepare the meat so it can be cooked at a high heat without setting off your fire alarms. You may have a good quality butcher to do this for you, but in case you don't, we explain the procedure for you. Pre-salting the filet is not necessary, but will enhance the flavor of this mild cut of beef.

Virginia Taylor
Geoff 2006
Anna 2007
Katie 2011

Serves 10 or up to 20 as part of a buffet

Filet

1 whole filet mignon (Costco's meat works fine)
Kosher salt
String for tying
2 tablespoons olive oil, plus extra for rubbing on the meat

200

Port Wine Sauce

¼ cup chopped shallots
1 sprig thyme
½ bottle ruby port, about 2 cups
3 cups veal stock, frozen Perfect Additions or homemade, not canned
½ cup cream

Wash and dry the filet. Notice the shape of the filet: the tail end tapers to a flat piece of meat, and the larger head portion is at the other end. Find the top of the filet, which has a continuous piece of fat and sinew, and the bottom, which has its fat incorporated into the meat. Find the rope of fatty meat that is attached to the side of the filet and loosen it with your fingers. With a sharp knife, remove the rope almost to the head of the filet. You will notice when this rope becomes more attached and is less fatty. You can save the rope for ground beef or chili. With your fingers or a knife, remove the fat on the top of the filet. Once the fat is removed, continue on with the sinew. With the tip of your knife, go under the layer of sinew that also covers the top of the filet and remove in strips by holding the blade at an angle against the sinew. Remove all of the sinew. Remove the fat that lies between the lobes of the head, being careful not to cut through the lobes. (The lobes will be opened but you will tie them closed later.) Turn the filet over to its back and slice some of the larger clumps of fat that are attached.

Do not remove all the fat, just the larger clumps. You may find that you need to remove a piece of the tail because of the fat it contains.

Now you are ready to pre-salt the filet. Using 1 teaspoon of kosher salt (½ teaspoon table salt) for each pound of meat, equally salt the filet, rubbing the salt into the meat. After you have salted the meat, it is necessary to tie it for even cooking.

Place the filet in front of you and fold the tail end under to create a more even roast. Cut your string into even lengths that are long enough to tie

(continued)

the meat around its circumference. You will need at least 10 to 12 pieces of string. Starting at the tail end, tightly tie the string around the tail to hold the piece you folded over in place as close to the end as you can. From there, go to the head end, tying each piece of string as tightly as you can at 1½-inch intervals until you reach the head. Make sure to tie the lobes carefully to the body to make a nice compact unit that will cook evenly. Now you can wrap the tied, salted filet in saran wrap and foil for the pre-salt marinade.

Let the meat sit for at least 24 hours (up to 2 days) wrapped in saran wrap then foil. The meat will release its juice then reabsorb the salted liquid to completely flavor the meat. This step is optional, but highly recommended.

Preheat the oven to 450 degrees.

Bring the filet to room temperature and dry well with paper towels. Rub the filet with olive oil. Preheat a large skillet over high heat. Add the olive oil and meat, reduce heat to medium-high and sear the meat on all sides. You may need to bend the filet to have it fit in the skillet or just sear half of it at a time, leaving the other portion hanging over the edge. (It works!) Save the skillet for making the sauce. Place the filet on a roasting pan and roast in a preheated oven for 20 to 25 minutes for medium rare, which is 120 degrees on an instant read thermometer.

While the meat is cooking, prepare the sauce. In the skillet used to cook the meat, add the shallots and brown for about 5 minutes, adding olive oil if needed. Add the port wine and thyme and reduce by one half. Add the veal stock and, over medium-high heat, reduce again, until the sauce is reduced by half and is flavorful. Add cream and continue reducing until the sauce has consistency and is more flavorful. Timing will depend on your heat. The higher the heat, the quicker it will take; however, there is more of a chance of over-reducing the sauce and burning it on a high heat. Take your time and do not be afraid to continuously reduce this sauce. The flavor is developed through the process of reduction and if it does not taste good, it is not reduced enough. You will not need salt to flavor this sauce. You should end up with no more than about ¾ cup of sauce; a little goes a long way.

Take the meat out of the oven after 20 minutes and use an instant read meat thermometer to test the meat. It should be at 120 degrees for medium rare. Let the meat rest for at least 10 minutes (half of its cooking time) before slicing to let the meat reabsorb its juices. Remove string and slice the filet into serving sized portions and serve with the port wine sauce.

Filet Mignon Roulade with Pine Nuts and Raisins

Virginia Taylor was taught this dish by a traditional Italian chef on the Amalfi Coast. In their wine cave beneath the restaurant, the first row was wine bottles filled with the fresh tomato sauce used for this dish. The combination of freshly puréed tomatoes with the wilted escarole and medium-rare meat filled with sweet raisins and nuts is unforgettable.

Virginia Taylor
Geoff 2006
Anna 2007
Katie 2011

Serves 6

Roulade

1½ pounds filet mignon, well trimmed and sliced into 6 thin pieces
Salt and pepper to taste
4 garlic cloves, minced
Extra-virgin olive oil
¾ cup pine nuts toasted, and chopped
¾ cup raisins, chopped
½ cup parsley, chopped
3 cups tomato sauce (recipe included)
Wilted escarole (recipe included)

Flatten the thin filet into as much of a rectangle as you can. Season both sides with salt and pepper. Sprinkle with a little garlic and rub with olive oil. Sprinkle the pine nuts, raisins and parsley evenly over each fillet. Even the long sides of the filet by folding each side in a little. Roll up the filet by starting with the short end. Secure with a toothpick.

Preheat oven to 400 degrees.

Heat a pan on medium-high heat, add about a tablespoon of olive oil and sear the roulades on each side. Place in an ovenproof pan. May be made one day ahead and refrigerated until serving time. Bring to room temperature before proceeding.

Finish cooking the beef roulades in the preheated oven for 8 minutes. Let sit for 2 minutes before slicing on a diagonal as you would an egg roll.

For the presentation, spoon the tomato sauce onto a plate to cover the surface. In the center of the plate, add a mound of the prepared escarole. Place the meat standing showing off the cut sides using the escarole to prop it up in the center of the plate.

Wilted Escarole

2 large yellow onions, sliced thinly in half moons
2 tablespoons butter
3 tablespoons olive oil
2 large heads of escarole, sliced
½ cup raisins, chopped
½ cup toasted pine nuts, chopped

Caramelize the onions in the butter and oil over very low heat. This will take at least an hour and up to two hours. Stir periodically. You can start the onion over a higher heat until limp (do not brown) then turn the heat down to low to finish the caramelization. Can be made ahead.

Once caramelized, increase heat and add the escarole; sauté until wilted. Add droplets of water, if you feel you need them. Add raisins and pine nuts then salt and pepper to taste.

(continued)

An easier version would omit caramelizing the onions. Instead, just sauté the onions over medium heat in the butter and olive oil until well cooked but not brown, about 15 minutes. Then add the escarole and finish the recipe as above. You can prepare the onions ahead of time and add the escarole at the last minute.

Tomato Sauce

5 pounds Farmer's Market tomatoes or sweet 100's if out of season, chopped
1 cup good quality olive oil
Salt
Balsamic Vinegar
Sugar

Heat the olive oil in a large sauté pan over medium-high heat until hot. Add tomatoes and sauté until they begin to release their juice. Lower the heat and cook for 15 minutes, stirring periodically.

Place the tomatoes through the small holes of a food mill to remove the seeds and skins or process in a food processor or blend with an emulsion blender and push through a strainer. Return sauce to the pan and reduce if necessary. Balance the flavor with the salt and balsamic vinegar. Add sugar if the tomatoes are too tart. This can be prepared two days in advance.

This sauce freezes beautifully since you might have leftovers.

Tester's Comments: *I served this dish with a clean, well balanced California Merlot and everything was an epicurean delight. The escarole, the tomato sauce and roulade, as a combination, was absolutely wonderful. It was well worth the effort. My husband has already requested this dish for his birthday dinner!*

Mary Pham

Joanie's Marinade
for Flank Steak

This is a must-have recipe for those who like teriyaki or satays. Joanie is a good friend of the Light/Kovachy family, and is the source of many of their favorite and most frequently used recipes. This particular marinade works equally well with chicken (breast or thighs). Just remember, this recipe takes an overnight marinade.

Susan Light
Tim Kovachy 2005
Benny Kovachy 2010

Serves 6

¼ cup soy sauce
3 tablespoons honey
2 tablespoons rice wine vinegar
2 cloves garlic, crushed
1 green onion, chopped
½ cup canola oil
Salt and pepper to taste
1 whole flank steak, 2 skirt steaks or 2 whole chicken breasts

In a bowl just large enough to hold the meat or chicken, add the soy sauce, honey, rice wine vinegar, garlic and green onion. Whisk in the canola oil and season with salt and pepper. Place meat or chicken in the marinade and refrigerate for at least 8 hours, preferably overnight.

When ready to cook, pat the meat dry and grill on the stovetop or barbecue with gas or charcoal until cooked to your liking (6 minutes per side for the flank steak for medium rare). Let meat sit for at least 5 minutes before slicing to allow the juice to reabsorb into the meat.

Braised Short Ribs
with Chocolate and Rosemary

Hints of rosemary and chocolate lend a subtle complexity to the rich, hearty sauce of this dish, without overpowering the tender meat of the short ribs. The entire dish can be prepared in advance, and is excellent served with rice, mashed potatoes, polenta or whipped sweet potatoes.   This recipe is adapted from *Bon Appétit*, January 2006, by Bruce Aidells and Nancy Oakes.

Lila Fitzgerald
Connor 2011

Serves 6 to 8

¼ cup diced pancetta (about 1½ ounces)
6 to 7 pounds bone-in short ribs, cut into 4 to 5-inch pieces
1½ cups finely chopped onions
¼ cup finely chopped shallots
¼ cup finely chopped celery
¼ cup peeled, finely chopped carrots
3 cloves garlic, minced
2 cups dry red wine
3 cups low-sodium chicken broth
2 cups canned tomatoes, drained and chopped
2 tablespoons chopped fresh parsley
1 to 2 large fresh thyme sprigs
1 bay leaf
2 tablespoons unsweetened cocoa powder (preferably Dutch process)
1 teaspoon finely chopped fresh rosemary

Heat heavy large pot over medium heat. Add pancetta and sauté until crisp, adding a tablespoon of olive oil if not enough fat is rendered. Using a slotted spoon, transfer pancetta to paper towels to drain. Sprinkle ribs with salt and pepper. Working in batches, brown ribs in drippings in the pot (adding olive oil as needed) over medium-high heat until brown on all sides, about 8 minutes per batch. Transfer to plate. Add onions, shallots, celery, carrots and garlic to pot; cover. Reduce heat to medium and cook about 10 minutes, stirring occasionally until vegetables are soft. Add wine to pot and bring to a boil, scraping up any browned bits. Boil uncovered until liquid is reduced by half, about 5 minutes. Reduce heat and add broth, tomatoes, parsley, thyme, bay leaf and pancetta. Return ribs to pot, cover partially, and simmer 1½ hours. Uncover and simmer, stirring occasionally, 1½ to 2 hours longer, until rib meat is tender.

Remove pot from heat, let cool slightly, and discard bay leaf. Separate ribs from sauce and refrigerate both overnight. Next day: remove all visible fat from sauce and meat. Bring sauce to a boil over medium-high heat until beginning to thicken. Reduce heat and add cocoa powder and rosemary, stirring until chocolate melts and is combined. Use an immersion blender to smooth sauce, if desired. Season to taste with salt and pepper. Return ribs to pot and simmer to warm, about 5 minutes.

Tester's Comments: *I found that a plain iron skillet worked better than the enameled pot for yielding a good, rich brown on the meat. So I used the skillet, added some wine to get the brown bits off, and transferred that to the main pot with the rest of the liquids. If you do not have an immersion blender, you can smooth the sauce by taking out most of the vegetables and enough of the liquid to fill a blender about ¾ of the way full, and blending together. The sauce will thicken and intensify in flavor as it cooks down, so I recommend waiting until the end to salt.*

Carolyn Dobervich

Barbeque Beef

Patty Turnquist shares this recipe, a family favorite, which dates back to when her grandparents owned a drugstore in Berwyn, Illinois, during the 1930s and 1940s. Her grandmother ran the lunch counter/soda fountain, and the Thursday special was always grandmother's recipe for barbequed-beef, served hot on a sandwich roll. While other types of beef will work, the preferred meat is tri-tip. Generally, any choice of meat should shred easily when still warm, before the fat has started to solidify again. This dish freezes well, and is quick and easy to make especially with the modern convenience of using a microwave to cook the beef. Enjoy!

Patty Turnquist
Eric 2012

Serves 8

2 ½ to 3 pounds beef (rump, chuck roast or tri-tip)
½ cup water
1 (14 ounce bottle) ketchup
2 tablespoons apple cider vinegar
1 green pepper, chopped
1 medium onion, diced
1 tablespoon sugar
1 teaspoon salt
1 teaspoon allspice
1 teaspoon mustard (yellow or Dijon)
1 small bunch celery, chopped

Place meat in microwaveable dish. Add approximately ½ cup water and partially cover the meat with plastic wrap. Cook meat at 50 percent power until cooked through, about 20 minutes per pound. Cool meat until it is cool enough to handle, but still warm. Hand shred the meat into a large bowl. The meat can also be cooked in a standard oven and then shredded.

In a separate bowl, combine the ketchup, cider vinegar, green pepper, onion, sugar, salt, allspice, mustard and celery and then add to the meat. Mix well and refrigerate overnight, allowing the flavors to blend together.

May be served hot or cold.

Tester's Comments: *I ended up cooking the meat in the microwave for 43 minutes, but that will vary according to the amount and the microwave. I broke the meat into chunks with a fork immediately after I removed it from the microwave, and then hand-shredded it as it cooled; it shredded just fine. I served this dish hot, open faced, on good crusty white bread, with a side salad.*

Susan Dennis

Meatloaf
with a Sweet and Sour Glaze

The only thing we can say about this recipe is make sure you double it—you will definitely want leftovers for sandwiches the next day! While this version calls for a combination of meats, it is still delicious with just ground beef. Derived from the *Spice Islands Cookbook* in 1961, this version is so much better than your mother used to make.

Wayne and Cindy Davison
Amanda 2000
Andy 2008

Serves 6

Glaze

6 tablespoons brown sugar
6 tablespoons red wine vinegar
1 teaspoon Dijon mustard
4 teaspoons Worcestershire sauce

Meatloaf

8-ounce can tomato sauce
1½ cups breadcrumbs, made from fresh cubed bread processed in the food
    processor
2 tablespoons chopped green or red bell peppers
½ cup minced onions
1 teaspoon Beau Monde Seasoning
1½ teaspoons salt
½ teaspoon dried oregano
¼ teaspoon crushed red pepper flakes

¼ teaspoon fresh finely ground black pepper
1 large egg, beaten
1 pound lean ground beef
¼ pound ground pork
¼ pound ground veal

For the glaze, combine the brown sugar, vinegar, mustard and Worcestershire sauce; mix well. Feel free to double the sauce. Set aside.

Preheat oven to 350 degrees.

Place breadcrumbs in large mixing bowl. Warm tomato sauce in a small saucepan and pour over breadcrumbs; stir to combine. Mix in green or red peppers, onions, Beau Monde, salt, oregano, red pepper flakes, black pepper and egg; combine well. Add the ground beef, pork and veal to the breadcrumbs and seasonings and mix thoroughly.

Shape meat into loaf and place on a flat roasting pan. Bake, uncovered, for 1 hour. Remove from the oven, pour off accumulated fat and baste with glaze. Return to the oven for 30 more minutes, basting every 5 to 10 minutes with glaze. Let rest for 5 minutes before slicing.

Yummy BBQ Ribs

Everybody has their favorite way to make barbecued ribs, but we think the Quinn family version tops them all. Marinating the ribs overnight and then baking them before grilling creates a moist rib, full of flavor. Stellie Quinn freezes the ribs in the sauce ahead of time then brings them up on trips to Lake Tahoe for a quick, easy and delicious dinner.

Stellie Quinn
Cory 2011

Serves 4

2 cups pineapple juice
½ cup ketchup
2 tablespoons soy sauce
2 tablespoons honey
2 pounds baby back pork ribs

Combine pineapple juice, ketchup, soy sauce and honey in a saucepan. Simmer for 8 minutes to thicken. Cool.

Cover ribs with the cooled marinade and refrigerate for 8 hours or overnight.

Preheat oven to 350 degrees.

Bake the ribs in a preheated oven for 1 hour, basting occasionally until cooked through. Can be prepared to this step and finished later.

Finish the ribs on the grill, 3 inches from the heat source, over medium heat.

Grill about 4 to 5 minutes per side, basting with the remaining marinade or your favorite BBQ sauce.

Tester's Comments: *I recommend saving at least a ½ cup of sauce before you marinate the rib, to serve with the cooked ribs. We reheated the extra sauce after the ribs were cooked and everyone enjoyed that as their BBQ sauce.*

Carol Fischer

Pork Tenderloin
with Apricot Chutney

This easy, yet elegant entrée will impress your family. The chutney sauce is not too sweet and is complemented with the pleasant, subtle ginger taste. The mustard seed gives a lovely hint of spice, and the suspended seeds give a nice look to the sauce. The chutney itself will keep for up to 3 weeks in the refrigerator in an airtight container, and is great served cold as a dipping sauce for pork or chicken.

Lisa Plain
Hap 2006
Alex 2008

Serves 4

1 pound pork tenderloin, trimmed of fat and silver skin
2 teaspoons butter
⅓ cup apricot chutney (recipe follows)
⅓ cup water
Salt and pepper

Preheat oven to 400 degrees.

Make apricot chutney and set aside.

Melt butter in ovenproof sauté pan (preferably nonstick). Add tenderloin and brown well on all sides (5 to 6 minutes).

Add chutney and water to pan, to incorporate drippings. Baste tenderloin with sauce and place in preheated oven. Roast, basting often, until meat reaches 145 degrees at its thickest point, about 20 minutes. Transfer to platter and pour the sauce in pan over pork. Let sit for at least 5 minutes, allowing meat to absorb its juices. Slice and serve with remaining chutney.

Apricot Chutney

1½ cups apricot jam
1 cup rice wine vinegar
⅓ cup mustard seed
1 tablespoon minced fresh ginger

Combine jam, vinegar, mustard seed and ginger in a small saucepan. Over medium heat, bring to a boil, stirring often. Boil at medium-low for about 8 minutes until reduced to sauce consistency. Will thicken as it cools. May be kept 2 to 3 weeks, refrigerated, in an airtight container.

Tester's Comments: *Since I transferred the tenderloin to a glass baking dish for the oven cooking, my sauce began to burn at the high temperature. I lowered the heat to 375 degrees, added a tablespoon more water and turned my tenderloin 3 times for even browning. Just remember to keep an eye on the meat.*

Georgia Baba

Italian Rosemary and Olive Garlic Pork Roast

The pork baking in your oven with the rosemary, garlic and olive tapenade will make your entire home smell of Tuscany. Perfect as a spring meal with roasted new potato fingerlings and steamed asparagus. Linda's boys love this meal any time of the year.

Linda Bader
Scott Bader 2006
Brett Bader 2012

Serves 6

3 slices pancetta
1 loin of pork roast (about 4 ½ pounds)
2 garlic cloves, sliced thin
6 tablespoons olive paste (recipe follows)
¼ cup small leaf clusters from fresh rosemary sprigs
¼ cup water
1 tablespoon chopped fresh parsley leaves
Fresh rosemary and parsley sprigs for garnish

Preheat oven to 350 degrees.

Trim fat on pork roast to ¼ inch thick. With a paring knife make shallow slits in the fat about 1 inch apart and in each insert a garlic slice and a rosemary leaf cluster. Spread the olive paste over the roast and place the slices of pancetta on top of the roast. Season the roast with salt and freshly ground black pepper. Place ¼ cup water in the bottom of the roasting pan and roast the pork for 1 hour and 20 minutes, or until roast registers 160 degrees on a meat thermometer. Transfer the pork to a platter and let stand 15 minutes before carving. Slice pork and arrange on a platter garnished with rosemary and parsley sprigs.

218

Olive Tapenade

½ cup picoline olives
4 tablespoons fresh basil, chopped
3 garlic cloves, mashed to a paste *with* ½ teaspoon salt
1 cup chopped fresh parsley leaves
¼ cut extra virgin olive oil
2 tablespoons freshly grated Parmesan

In a food processor puree the olives, basil, garlic paste and parsley. With the motor running, add the oil in a stream and then the Parmesan and blend the mixture well.

Makes about 1 cup

Buttermilk Brined Pork Chops

Ideal for parents on the go, this is a quick and easy weeknight meal but special enough for dinner party. Brining the pork chops in buttermilk overnight flavors the pork and makes it very tender. Just remember to buy your pork chops the day before!

Betsy Haehl
Alicia Kriewall 2007

Serves 4

2 cups fat-free buttermilk
2 tablespoons kosher salt
2 tablespoons sugar
1 tablespoon grated lemon rind
1 teaspoon chopped fresh rosemary
1 teaspoon chopped fresh sage
4 center cut pork chops, about 1½-inch thick (thinner, bone-in chops will
    do, but reduce cooking time)
2 teaspoons freshly ground black pepper
Melted butter or cooking spray

In a large zip-top plastic bag, add the buttermilk, salt, sugar, lemon rind, rosemary and sage; shake well to dissolve salt and sugar. Add pork. Seal and refrigerate overnight, turning bag occasionally. Remove pork from bag; discard brine. Pat the pork completely dry with a paper towel. Sprinkle pork with pepper.

Preheat broiler.

You can either pan grill or broil the chops. Broil on one side for 5 minutes;

baste with butter and broil the other side for an additional 5 to 6 minutes or until slightly pink in the center.

To pan cook, heat a large, nonstick grill pan over medium-high heat. Coat the pan with cooking spray. Add pork and cook on each side until desired degree of doneness, about 6 minutes on each side.

For both methods, let the chops rest for a few minutes, covered loosely, before serving.

⌇

Tester's Comments: *This is a real keeper! It's foolproof and a crowd pleaser. We served it for dinner when we had people over and both the adults and kids absolutely loved it! We broiled ours but next time we'll try barbecuing the chops.*

Kevin Corkery

Lamb Patties Picatta

Refreshing additions to your recipe repertoire, Lamb Patties Piccata and Chicken Patties with Fresh Herbs (page 188) provide quick and easy meals utilizing ground meats. The use of herbs and lemon zest adds an unusual and delicious twist to a standard meat patty. Add Fragrant Barley Casserole (page 254), Wheat Pilaf (page 253) or couscous with some wilted greens for a perfect mid week dinner.

Irina Sarkisov
Katya 2006

Serves 4

1 pound lean ground lamb
¼ cup plus 2 tablespoons minced parsley, divided
¼ cup plain, dried bread crumbs
¼ cup cold water
1 tablespoon freshly grated lemon peel
2 teaspoons minced garlic
¾ teaspoon salt
3 tablespoons fresh lemon juice
2 teaspoons butter
1 tablespoon olive oil
Instant read meat thermometer (optional)

Mix lamb, ¼ cup parsley, breadcrumbs, cold water, lemon peel, garlic and salt in a bowl until well blended. Shape into four, 4-inch patties.

Heat sauté pan over medium-high heat; add olive oil. Lower heat to medium and cook patties about 5 to 6 minutes per side until an instant read thermometer, inserted from side to center, registers 150 degrees. Remove and transfer to a serving plate. Cover loosely with foil.

Drain fat from skillet. Stir in lemon juice and 1 tablespoon water. Bring to a boil. Add butter, stirring to melt, and blend. Remove from heat. Stir in 2 tablespoons parsley and pour over patties.

⁓

Tester's Comments: *I wanted more sauce to dress my barley side dish, so after I cooked the patties, I added ¼ cup of shallots to the skillet without draining the fat. I put in 2 teaspoons of flour to help bind the sauce, cooked it for a minute, and then added ¼ cup white wine and reduced that by half over medium-high heat. I then added 1 cup of chicken stock and reduced that to sauce consistency, about 2 to 4 minutes, on medium-high heat. Next I added 2 tablespoons of lemon juice and the parsley. For a bit of extra flair, I threw in a few capers. It was absolutely delicious!*

Virginia Taylor

Rack of Lamb
with Mint Vinaigrette

This vinaigrette, from Wolfgang Puck, was originally suggested with chicken satays but to us, mint and lamb goes hand in hand. You can serve this with Cabbage Rice (page 251) and Aegean Salad (page 64)—just pour the mint vinaigrette over everything. The flavor combination will make it a family favorite even for those who thought they did not like lamb!

Virginia Taylor
Geoff 2006
Anna 2007
Katie 2011

Serves 6

2 racks of lamb, fat completely removed, seasoned with salt and olive oil
1 tablespoon olive oil
1 small bunch fresh mint (about 1 cup) lightly packed, stems removed
1 egg yolk
¼ cup seasoned rice wine vinegar
1 tablespoon soy sauce
½ teaspoon ground coriander
½ cup peanut oil
¼ teaspoon freshly ground pepper

Preheat oven to 400 degrees.

Heat a large sauté pan over medium-high heat, add oil and, when just smoking, add the lamb, flesh side down and sear well. Turn over to the bone side and sear again. Place on a roasting pan bone side down. Bake for 20 to 25 minutes until the meat registers 120 on an instant read thermometer. Cover loosely with foil and let rest for at least 10 minutes before cutting.

To barbecue, preheat grill to medium and place lamb bone side down on grill; cover. Grill for 10 to 12 minutes, turn to the flesh side and grill until meat tests at 120 degrees, about 10 more minutes. Cover and let rest for 10 minutes.

While meat is cooking make the vinaigrette. In a blender or food processor, combine mint, yolk, vinegar, soy sauce and coriander with a little oil. With the motor running, slowly pour in the remaining oil and blend until smooth. Refrigerate, covered, until needed.

Cut rack into individual serving pieces by slicing the meat between each bone. Pour a bit of vinaigrette onto the lamb and serve with vinaigrette on the side.

Recipe Note: Pape Meat Company in Milbrae has the most perfectly prepared racks of lamb on the Peninsula. Mike takes every bit of fat from the rack leaving only that delectable nugget of meat hugging the bones. With the layer of fat gone, the racks can even go directly on the barbecue without worry of flair ups. They come seasoned or plain, and both are perfect for this recipe. It is worth the trip to Milbrae to get your lamb for this recipe—and get a few extra for later! Mike will vacuum pack your extras to go straight into the freezer.

Dad's Dog Breath Chili

Have plenty of water handy! This spicy chili is guaranteed to make you pant like a dog! Paul Hickman lost the original recipe years ago, so he found a recipe on the Internet and used it in conjunction with what he remembered from the original. Some of the ingredients can be hard to find, and it is recommended that you call ahead to a specialty or gourmet food market for items like the dried peppers and the specific chili powders.

Paul Hickman
James 2009

Serves 8

3 dried Chipotle peppers
1 dried Habanero pepper
5 dried Cascabel (Arbol) peppers
8 ounces regular breakfast sausage (bulk or, if using links, sliced)
2 tablespoons vegetable oil, and more as needed for frying
2 pounds tri-tip beef, cut in small cubes
1 pound lamb, cut in small cubes
1 (14 ounce can) beef broth
1 (14 ounce can) chicken broth, plus additional if needed
1 medium onion, finely chopped
¼ teaspoon dried oregano
3 tablespoons cumin, divided
7 cloves garlic, peeled and chopped
1 tablespoon hot chili powder
1 tablespoon mild chili powder
1 tablespoon chili con carne powder
5 tablespoons red chili powder
1 (8 ounce can) tomato sauce
1 (14.5 ounce can) Hunt's diced tomatoes with chilies

½ teaspoon cayenne pepper
1 teaspoon Tabasco pepper sauce
1 teaspoon brown sugar
Juice of 1 lime
Salt to taste
½ bottle of beer
1 dash whiskey
1½ pounds dried pinto beans, cooked according to package directions (optional)

Clean the stems and seeds from the Chipotle, Habanero and Cascabel peppers, using surgical gloves to protect your hands. Bring a small saucepan of water to a boil. Remove water from heat, add chili peppers and place a lid one size smaller than the pan into the water to submerge the peppers. Soak peppers in hot water until soft, about 1 hour. Purée softened peppers in a blender or food processor with a little of the soaking liquid until a smooth paste is created.

Brown the sausage, drain and set aside. Heat oil in a large heavy pot over medium-high heat and sear the beef and lamb in batches until nicely browned. Add the remaining meat, cooked sausage, onion, beef and chicken broths to the pot; adding broth if necessary to cover the meat. Bring to a boil and cook, uncovered, over medium heat for 15 minutes.

Add oregano and 1½ tablespoons of the cumin. Reduce heat to a light boil and then add the garlic.

In a separate bowl, combine the four chili powders together; add half to the pot (reserve the rest) and cook 15 minutes, uncovered.

Add tomato sauce, tomatoes with chilies and the puréed pepper mixture. Thin with chicken broth to the desired consistency, if needed. Cook, covered, for one hour over a low simmer, stirring often.

Add ½ bottle beer (Heineken preferred), a dash of whiskey (preferably Jack

(continued)

Daniels), 1½ tablespoon reserved cumin and the remaining chili powder mixture and simmer for another 25 minutes on low heat, covered.
Add pinto beans if using. Bring pot up to a light boil and add the Tabasco, cayenne pepper, brown sugar, lime juice and salt. Let flavors blend for a few minutes at a light boil, uncovered. Correct the seasonings, adding salt, brown sugar and additional lime to taste.

Serve in bread bowls or with corn bread.

Notes from the chef: This chili is very spicy. For a milder chili, substitute dried Chipotle peppers for the Habanero and mild chili powder for the hot. We get all the dried peppers at Draeger's. The brand is Los Chileros de Nuevo Mexico and they are in the gourmet international food section. The dried peppers impart a roasted flavor and also a stronger intensity. Cascabel peppers are also called Arbol chili peppers.

Tester's Comments: *The recipe is time consuming, but it freezes well and can be reheated for a hearty, flavorful dinner in minutes. I actually brought our frozen leftovers, reheated in a crockpot, to our yacht club's chili cookoff and placed it before a large group of very discerning judges. It made a respectable showing with a fourth place prize!*

Patty Turnquist

Pasta, Rice, Grains

Furred and Feathered Residents

In the early morning chill of a school day during the first week of October, Father Maurus blesses any and all pets brought to him in honor of St. Francis of Assisi. While the annual Blessing of the Pets attracts a variety of visiting beasts—from a lizard or a hamster in a cage, to dogs, cats and the occasional horse or donkey on the hoof—there have also been many resident animals at the Priory over the years. These resident pets must have a strong sense of self-preservation because the coyotes that lurk in the hills are always on the prowl.

Fluffy the dorm cat was one survivor of the rigors of outdoor life in Portola Valley. Although no one ever discovered exactly where Fluffy spent the night, during the day she could be found sleeping in Founders Hall or making the rounds at the back doors of the dining hall or the monastery looking for a handout. In her later years, she learned that some of the ladies who attend the Hungarian Mass on Sunday morning would often bring her a treat. One day, impatient for her admirers to emerge from the chapel, she wandered down the middle of the aisle during Mass and curled up in front of the altar!

The Priory also became home for a time to a small flock of chickens that had been left at the San Mateo Humane Society. Most of these fowl succumbed to the coyotes in fairly short order, but one crafty rooster, George, learned to roost high in the trees at night and lived long enough to become lonely. A compassionate student brought a hen—soon to be named Georgina—to keep George company, and the two chickens enjoyed their Priory paradise, finding bugs to eat and the occasional bit of kitchen food left out for them by Father Maurus. George announced the coming of each new day, as roosters do, and was admired by all of the human residents on campus, even the dormers who might be awakened early by his shrill alarm. Indeed, George and Georgina were a charming addition to our rural campus.

Baked Penne
with Sausage and Broccoli

Betsy Haehl learned this recipe in a cooking class given by Joanne Weir, which must have been themed "make ahead," because the recipe creates the perfect potluck dish. The entire meal—meat, starch and vegetable—is in this recipe, and it can be prepared entirely ahead of time with a 40 minute visit in the oven to finish it off. It would also make a perfect vegetarian dish if you substitute mushrooms for the sausage and use vegetable broth.

Betsy Haehl
Alicia Kriewall 2007

Serves 8

1½ pounds Italian sausage (hot or mild, or a combination of both), casings removed
1 tablespoon olive oil
1 onion, chopped
2 cloves garlic, minced
1 (28 ounce can) imported tomatoes, chopped, reserve liquid
½ cup dry red wine
½ cup beef stock, plus additional
½ teaspoon dried oregano
½ teaspoon dried thyme
¼ cup chopped parsley
¾ pounds of penne, cooked and drained
1½ bunches broccoli, cut into small pieces and blanched until just tender
1 pound whole-milk Mozzarella (dried or fresh), diced
½ cup grated Parmesan cheese

Preheat the oven to 350 degrees.

Heat a large skillet over medium-high heat; add olive oil and sausage, breaking it up with the back of your spoon. After the sausage has rendered some of its fat, add the onion and garlic and cook until soft, about 5 minutes. Drain off excess fat, if desired. Stir in tomatoes with their juice, wine, stock, and the oregano, thyme and parsley. Bring to a boil, lower the heat, cover and simmer for 20 minutes.

While the pasta sauce is cooking, boil the pasta. In a large pot, bring 6 quarts of water to a boil and then add 2 tablespoons salt. Add the penne and cook until al dente, about 10 to 12 minutes.

Toss the penne with the sausage mixture, broccoli and mozzarella in a large bowl. Pour mixture into a large baking dish, sprinkle with Parmesan cheese and add a bit more beef broth. Bake about 40 minutes; 30 minutes covered with foil, removing foil for last 10 minutes, until bubbly.

Penne
with Olives, Capers and Feta

This cold pasta salad, from Tracy Kraczkowsky's good friend and fabulous cook Connie Ives, is the perfect meal for a hot summer night or a light luncheon. The flavors are classic: salty olives and cheese, sweet tomatoes and peppers, briny capers and sharp onions. Allow this salad to marinate in the refrigerator for several hours before serving to let the flavors develop, adding the cheese right before mealtime.

Tracy Kraczkowsky
Colin 2009

Serves 8

12 ounces dry penne rigate pasta
2 tablespoons salt
7 tablespoons olive oil, divided
7 tablespoons red wine vinegar
2 cloves garlic, minced
Freshly ground salt and pepper
1 tablespoon chopped fresh oregano
1 cup thinly sliced red onion
¾ cup pitted Kalamata olives, coarsely chopped
5 tablespoons capers, drained
1 small red bell pepper, thinly sliced
1 small yellow bell pepper, thinly sliced
1 pint Sweet 100 cherry tomatoes (red, yellow or a mix) or grape tomatoes, halved or quartered
8 ounces feta cheese, crumbled
Oregano sprigs for garnish

In a large pot, bring 6 quarts of water to a boil and then add 2 tablespoons salt. Add the penne and cook until al dente, about 10 to 12 minutes. Drain the pasta and toss it immediately with 1 tablespoon of the olive oil. Let it cool completely in the refrigerator.

In a large bowl, whisk the remaining 6 tablespoons olive oil with the vinegar and garlic. Season to taste with salt and pepper. Add oregano, onion, olives, capers, bell peppers and tomatoes to the penne and toss to distribute vegetables. Add the dressing and toss again to coat the pasta. At this point you can refrigerate the pasta for up to a few hours.

To serve, add the feta and stir until just combined.

⁓

Tester's Comments: *Our family made this recipe on a cold, rainy weekend in March, so for the second night we heated the pasta in the microwave for 5 minutes, added more feta as a garnish and served it with fresh-baked bread. We had a wonderful meal for four and this versatile recipe was equally good cold as it was warm.*

The Corkery Family

Curried Orzo Pasta
with Almonds and Currants

Orzo is a rice shaped pasta and can be found in the pasta section of most supermarkets. This dish is cooked in chicken broth to add flavor to the pasta itself, then added to the onions cooked in olive oil, curry and mango chutney. It's a perfect side dish to Turkey Picatta (page 174) or just a plain roasted chicken.

Virginia Taylor
Geoff 2006
Anna 2007
Katie 2011

Serves 8 as a side course

1 (48 ounce can) chicken stock
¼ teaspoon salt
1½ cups dried orzo pasta
¼ cup extra-virgin olive oil
1 medium onion, chopped
2 teaspoons curry powder
¼ teaspoon cumin
Pinch of red pepper flakes
1 tablespoon prepared mango chutney
½ cup dried currants
1 tablespoon chopped parsley
½ cup sliced almonds, toasted for 7 minutes in a 350-degree oven

Bring chicken stock to a boil in a medium saucepan. Add salt and orzo pasta and cook until pasta is al dente, about 8 minutes, stirring often. The pasta will absorb a good portion of the stock.

While the pasta is cooking, heat a medium-sized sauté pan over moderate heat. Add olive oil and onions and sauté for 1 minute. Add curry powder, cumin and pepper flakes, and sauté until the onion is translucent. Add the chutney and currants; stir well.

Drain the pasta and add it to the sauté pan with the onions. Add parsley; toss until well coated. Transfer to a serving dish and top with toasted almond. This dish can be made ahead of time up to this step, and reheated in a microwave oven. Add the toasted almonds right before serving.

Tester's Comments: *One of my kids, who is a picky eater, requested the leftovers for lunch the next day!*

Sharon Traeger

Bolognese

This sauce, from Food Network's *Everyday Italian*, is one of those classic dishes that truly does taste better the next day, making it a great make-ahead meal. The combination of onions, celery and carrot simmered together in olive oil with the ground beef, tomatoes and herbs is a simple gift to a perfectly cooked noodle. This is a great dish after a long day of skiing.

Marjorie Brent
Laura 2004
Ian 2007

Serves 8

¼ cup extra-virgin olive oil
1 medium onion, finely diced
2 cloves garlic, minced
1 stalk celery, finely diced
1 medium carrot, peeled and finely diced
1 pound ground beef (or a combination of beef, veal and pork)
1 (28 ounce can) crushed tomatoes
¼ cup fresh Italian parsley, chopped
8 leaves fresh basil, chopped
½ teaspoon salt
½ teaspoon freshly ground pepper, plus more to taste
¼ cup freshly grated Pecorino Romano cheese plus more for serving
1 pound pasta of your choice

In a large skillet heat the oil over a medium flame. When almost smoking, add the onion and garlic; sauté until onion is tender, about 8 minutes. Add the celery and carrot; sauté for 5 minutes. Increase the heat to high, add the ground beef and sauté until the meat is no longer pink, breaking up any large lumps, about 10 minutes. Add the tomatoes, parsley, basil, salt and pepper; cook over medium-low heat until the sauce thickens, about 30 minutes. Stir in cheese, then season with more salt and pepper as desired. (Sauce can be made 1 day ahead. Cool, then cover and refrigerate. Rewarm over medium-high heat before serving.)

When sauce is almost done, bring a large pot of water to a boil. Salt the water so it tastes like the sea and add the pasta, giving it a good stir. Bring the water back to a boil, cook until al dente, stirring periodically. Drain the pasta, saving at least a half cup of the pasta water. Place the pasta back in the pot and add the sauce stirring to coat the pasta. Add pasta water until there is a good consistency to the sauce. Reheat sauce and pasta over medium until hot and the pasta has absorbed some of the sauce, just a few minutes. Serve with extra cheese.

Pasta Sauce Raphel

Many years ago a dear friend of the Brent family became a vegetarian. When she would delight them with her company, Marjorie Brent was kind enough to cook strictly vegetarian meals. This recipe, from The New Basics Cookbook, was so wonderful that Marjorie began cooking it even when her friend was not visiting. Full of flavor and made with ingredients typically found in the pantry, this recipe remains one of her family's favorite and will soon become one of yours.

Marjorie Brent
Laura 2004
Ian 2007

Serves 6

2 (6 ounce jars) marinated artichoke hearts
¼ cup olive oil
2 cups chopped onions
2 tablespoons minced garlic
½ teaspoon dried oregano
½ teaspoon dried basil
1 tablespoon coarsely ground pepper
½ teaspoon salt
A pinch red pepper flakes
1 (28 ounce can) plum tomatoes, with their juice, crushed
¼ cup Parmesan cheese
¼ cup Italian parsley (optional), chopped
1 pound linguini or spaghetinni

Drain the artichoke hearts, reserving the marinade. Heat the olive oil in a large saucepan over medium-low heat. Add the onions, garlic, oregano, basil, black pepper, salt, red pepper flakes and reserved marinade. Sauté until the garlic and onions are translucent, about 10 minutes. Add the tomatoes and their juice and simmer for 30 minutes.

While the sauce is cooking, boil the pasta. In a large pot, bring 6 quarts of water to a boil and then add 2 tablespoons salt. Add the pasta and cook until al dente, about 10 to 12 minutes.

Add the artichoke hearts, Parmesan cheese and parsley (if desired) to the simmering sauce. Stir gently and simmer for 5 minutes. Serve over pasta.

Tester's Comments: *Since I am a carnivore, I served this with a grilled veal chop and saved some of the sauce to place on top of the meat. The meat, the pasta and that wonderful sauce was all that we needed along with a good bottle of red wine, of course!*

Virginia Taylor

Dordie's Creamy Tomato Pasta

Need an easy, hearty recipe to feed the entire soccer team you have coming over in 30 minutes? This creamy, cheesy tomato sauce is delicious, and Dordie, Ann Dingerson's friend, knew when she adapted this recipe from the *Open Hand Cookbook* that she had a winner on her hands. To incorporate your vegetables into this pasta, search your refrigerator for leftover green beans, broccoli or asparagus to throw in at the last minute. It's truly a refrigerator pasta!

The Corkery Family
Kelsey 2007
Teagan 2009

Serves 16

¾ cup butter (1 ½ sticks)
2 (28 ounce cans) plum tomatoes, drained and chopped (or blended in a
    food processor)
2 pounds rigatoni
24 basil leaves, coarsely chopped
¾ cup half & half
2 cups freshly grated Pecorino or Parmesan cheese
Salt and pepper to taste

Melt the butter in a large sauté pan with deep sides. Add the chopped tomatoes and cook for about 10 minutes over low to medium heat.

At the same time, bring a pot of water to a boil. Generously salt the water. Add the rigatoni and cook until it is about 4 minutes from being done.

244

Drain pasta, saving a cup of pasta water for the sauce, if needed.

Once drained, immediately add the rigatoni to the tomato mixture and cook over medium heat, stirring, for about 3 minutes. Add basil leaves, cream and cheese. Salt and pepper to taste. If the sauce seems too thick, thin by adding a little milk, additional half & half or reserved pasta water. Cook until the pasta is al dente.

Serve immediately with extra grated cheese. Or, if you want to make this ahead of time, transfer the mixture to a buttered casserole dish and reheat later in a 325-degree oven for about 30 minutes.

Tester's Comments: *My teenagers had the leftovers for breakfast the next day!*

Amy Magnuson

Saffron Risotto
with Vegetables du Jour

Want to make a great risotto in 8 minutes? Try cooking it in a pressure cooker, as recommended in *Great Vegetarian Cooking Under Pressure*, by Lorna J. Sass. Sharon Traeger has never again made her risotto with the normal pour-and-stir method and promises it tastes just the same. If you do not have a pressure cooker, follow the directions for Smoked Salmon Risotto with Whiskey and Dill (page 248). Whichever way you choose to cook it, this dish is delicious.

Sharon Traeger
Alix 2011

Serves 6 as a first course

1 tablespoon olive oil
½ cup finely chopped leeks (white and light green parts), shallots or onions
1½ cups Arborio rice
3½ to 4 cups vegetable stock
Generous ¼ teaspoon saffron threads
1 teaspoon salt, or to taste
1½ to 2 cups chopped cooked vegetables (carrots, beans, peas, zucchini, corn, etc.)
2 to 3 tablespoons minced fresh parsley
½ cup freshly grated Parmesan cheese (or 1-3 teaspoons balsamic vinegar or 1-3 tablespoons fresh squeezed lemon juice)
Freshly ground pepper to taste

Heat the oil in the cooker. Cook the leeks over medium-high heat, stirring frequently, for 1 minute. Add the rice, stirring to coat with oil. Add 3 ½ cups of the stock, the saffron and salt.

Lock the lid in place. Over high heat, bring to high pressure. Lower the heat just enough to maintain high pressure and cook for 5 minutes. Reduce the pressure with a quick-release method. Carefully remove the lid, tilting it away from you to allow any excess steam to escape.

Stir in the vegetables, parsley, and Parmesan cheese (if desired). For a more creamy risotto, stir in a bit more stock. Cook over medium heat, stirring constantly, until the rice achieves the desired consistency: it should be tender but chewy and the vegetables thoroughly heated. Stir in Parmesan cheese and pepper. Serve immediately in shallow soup bowls.

Smoked Salmon Risotto with Whiskey and Dill

This unusual risotto recipe from Virginia Taylor won the second place spot at the annual risotto cook-off for the Italian Museo in San Francisco. A true Italian would never put cheese in a risotto with fish, but Virginia is not Italian. The cheese makes the risotto salty and creamy enough to create the perfect first course. This risotto will be loose and to keep it that way, it is best served as soon as it is finished in shallow soup bowls.

Virginia Taylor
Geoff 2006
Anna 2007
Katie 2011

Serves 6 to 8 as a first course

5 cups chicken broth, canned is fine
1 tablespoon extra-virgin olive oil
4 tablespoons unsalted butter, divided
½ cup finely chopped shallots
1½ cups Arborio rice
½ cup dry white wine or Champagne

1 cup sliced smoked salmon, about 6 ounces
⅓ cup good quality whiskey
1 cup heavy cream
2 tablespoons chopped dill, plus additional for a garnish
½ cup freshly grated Parmigiano-Reggiano cheese, plus additional for garnish

Bring the broth to a simmer in a saucepan.

Heat oil and two tablespoons of butter in a heavy 4-quart pan over moderate heat. Add the shallots and sauté for 1 to 2 minutes until they begin to soften but are not yet brown. Using a wooden spoon, stir the rice into the onion mixture. Continue stirring for 1 minute, making sure all the grains are well coated. Add the wine and cook, stirring frequently, until the wine is absorbed. Begin to add the simmering broth, ½ cup to 1 cup at a time, again stirring frequently. Wait until each addition is almost absorbed before adding the next cup. Keep the risotto at an even, lively but low, boil to ensure the proper rate of evaporation of the broth. The entire addition of all the broth should take between 15 to 18 minutes.

While the risotto is cooking, make the smoked salmon sauce. In a medium-sized sauté pan, heat the remaining two tablespoons of butter over moderate heat. When melted and hot, add the salmon and stir-fry until almost opaque. Add whiskey, turn up the heat and reduce by half. Add the cream, bring to a boil and then add the dill. Remove the sauce from the heat and set aside in a warm place until ready to use.

Begin tasting the risotto after 15 minutes of cooking to determine if it is done. The timing may vary by 2 to 3 minutes on either side. You may not need all the broth. If you need more liquid, add hot water. (This will depend on your rice.) Once done, add the salmon sauce and stir to heat and incorporate into the rice. Add the cheese, stir and serve immediately in wide brimmed soup bowls. Garnish with additional dill and cheese.

Simple Herb Fried Rice

This recipe was developed by Mary Pham's son David, who is neither a fan of meat nor egg in his fried rice. This rice is simply seasoned with green onions, parsley and cilantro. It is a perfect accompaniment to trout, halibut or salmon. Feel free to add shrimp, chicken or other savory items to the rice as a variation.

Mary Pham
David Low 2010

Serves 6

2 tablespoons olive oil; more if needed
1 yellow onion, diced
5 green onions, sliced
1 cup Italian parsley, minced
1 cup cilantro, minced
3 cloves garlic, minced
4 cups of cold, cooked rice
Sea salt to taste
Freshly cracked pepper to taste

Heat oil in a frying pan over medium heat. Sauté yellow and green onions until translucent, being careful to avoid browning or burning the onions. Add parsley and cilantro, lowering heat if necessary; pour a bit more oil if needed to keep ingredients from sticking. Stir in garlic and rice, mixing well. Cook until rice is soft and hot, and all ingredients are well incorporated.

Cabbage Rice

This rice recipe is adapted from the wonderful Mediterranean cookbook *The Food of Greece*, by Aglaia Kremezi, and is one of the most flavorful, unusual rice dishes you will taste. The flavor comes from the olive oil, basmati rice, sweet onions and pinch of pepper flakes. It's a must with the Rack of Lamb with Mint Vinaigrette (page 224). The combination of the lamb and mint vinaigrette with the rice to soak up the flavors is truly divine.

Virginia Taylor
Geoff 2006
Anna 2007
Katie 2011

Serves 10

½ cup olive oil
2 medium onions, coarsely chopped (about 2 cups)
½ teaspoon salt
½ teaspoon dried red pepper flakes
2½ cups chopped green cabbage
1½ cups basmati rice
2½ cups chicken broth
2 tablespoons chopped dill (optional)

In a deep, heavy skillet with lid, heat the oil over medium heat and sauté the onions and salt until translucent, about 3 minutes. Add pepper flakes and cabbage; sauté for another 2 minutes until cabbage is wilted. Add rice and coat with oil.

While cooking onions and cabbage, heat the broth in a separate saucepan. When it starts to boil, pour it over the rice and reduce the heat. Mix well with a wooden spoon and cover; simmer for 18 minutes. Turn off heat, sprinkle on dill, replace the cover and let rest for at least 5 minutes. Mix well and serve.

Vermicelli Rice Pilaf

This classic recipe, from *Sunset Magazine*, is one that Patty Turnquist makes for her family nearly every week. It can be made earlier in the day then reheated in the microwave before serving. The 40 minute, do-not-disturb baking time allows plenty of time to prepare the other part of your dinner, such as Chicken with Currants (page 176), Jane's Fish Stew (page 142) or Squab with Grapes (page 162).

Patty Turnquist
Eric 2012

Serves 6

½ stick (4 tablespoons) butter or margarine
1 cup vermicelli broken into 1-inch lengths (angel hair, cappellini or any thin spaghetti type pasta works fine)
1 cup long grain converted rice
3 cups chicken broth, canned is fine
2 or 3 chopped scallions, both white and green parts

Place butter into a 2 ½- to 3-quart casserole and put in oven. Preheat oven to 350 degrees. Once oven has reached temperature, butter will be melted. Add broken vermicelli to casserole and stir to coat with melted butter. Return casserole to oven for approximately 10 minutes to lightly brown vermicelli.

While vermicelli is browning, heat chicken broth to boiling. Add rice to vermicelli and stir to coat. Pour boiling chicken broth over rice and vermicelli and stir to blend. Cover casserole and continue to cook in oven for 40 minutes, or until rice is tender and liquid has absorbed. Remove from oven, stir in the chopped scallions, cover and let rest for 5 minutes.

Wheat Pilaf

It's easy to forget how wonderful cooked whole grains are; however, this recipe will surely help you rediscover the healthy lower-carbohydrate alternative. Bulgar, or cracked wheat, is a delicious side dish, and, like rice, it is extremely versatile. Omit the currants and add grated zucchini and carrots at the end letting the heat steam them. Prefer a little celery? Just sauté it with the onions in the beginning. With this recipe, you can use your imagination and enjoy a lovely, nutritious starch substitute.

Margaret Herzen
Elena 2003
Juliana 2007

Serves 6

1 tablespoon extra-virgin olive oil
2 tablespoons minced onion
½ cup sliced mushrooms
½ cup currants
1 cup cracked wheat
2 cups chicken broth (canned is fine)
¼ teaspoon fresh chopped oregano
Salt and pepper to taste

Heat oil in a saucepan over medium heat. Sauté onions until soft. Add mushrooms and currants; sauté for another 3 to 4 minutes until mushrooms are cooked and have released their juices. Add cracked wheat and brown, stirring occasionally, for about 5 minutes. Pour in broth and add oregano, stirring to mix. Bring to a boil, lower heat to simmer, and then cover pot and cook until liquid is absorbed, about 15 to 20 minutes. At this point, if it is not dry and fluffy, remove lid and heat uncovered for a few minutes until dry.

Fragrant Barley Casserole

As a young bride in June of 1975, Margaret Herzen was eager to prepare healthy, yet tasty, dishes for her bicyclist spouse, she chanced by a cookbook called *Cooking With Gourmet Grains*, published by the Stone-Buhr Milling Company. Little did she know that 31 years later it would continue to be their favorite substitute for potatoes or rice. This side dish is lovely with Lamb Patties Picatta (page 222) or Meat Loaf with a Sweet and Sour Glaze (page 212).

Margaret Herzen
Elena 2003
Juliana 2007

Serves 6

1 tablespoon extra-virgin olive oil
1 tablespoon unsalted butter
1 cup sliced mushrooms
1 cup chopped onions
1½ cups pearl barley
3 cups low-sodium beef or chicken broth
¼ teaspoon salt
⅛ teaspoon pepper
½ cup chopped parsley

Preheat oven to 350 degrees.

In an ovenproof saucepan, melt olive oil and butter over medium heat. Add mushrooms and let cook, undisturbed until brown on one side, about 2 minutes. Add the onion and sauté until transparent, about 5 minutes. Add barley, sauté until slightly browned, about 5 more minutes, stirring frequently. Add broth and bring to a boil. Cover and place into preheated oven for about 20 minutes or until cooked but still slightly al dente. You may also cook this on the stovetop on low heat for the same amount of time.

Salt and pepper to taste. Just prior to serving, stir in the chopped parsley.

Tester's Comments: *This is a dish you can change with your mood. Use wild mushrooms instead of domestic. Add chopped celery and carrots with the onions for color and flavor. Add your leftover chicken, a little vinegar and a touch more olive oil for lunch the next day.*

Georgia Baba

Barley and Pine Nut Pilaf

Here is another version of barley but this one is spiked with pine nuts and green onions. This recipe is from Linda Bader's sister-in-law Patty Allen who inherited her mother's love for cooking and continues to re-create the recipes of her youth. This is just one of the many special comfort food recipes she has shared with Linda.

Linda Bader
Scott 2006
Brett 2012

Serves 6

1 cup pearl barley
6 tablespoons butter
2 ounces (⅓ cup) pine nuts
1 cup chopped green onions
½ cup chopped, fresh parsley or 2 ½ teaspoons dried
¼ teaspoon salt
¼ teaspoon pepper
3 ⅓ cups chicken broth

Preheat oven to 350 degrees.

Rinse barley in cold water and drain.

In a 10-inch skillet, heat butter over medium heat and saute pine nuts for about 5 minutes or until lightly brown. Remove with slotted spoon and reserve. Sauté green onions and barley in the same skillet until lightly toasted. Remove from heat. Stir in nuts, parsley, salt and pepper. Spoon into ungreased 2-quart casserole.

Heat broth to a boil and pour over barley mixture. Stir to blend well. Bake, uncovered, for 1 hour, 10 minutes. Fluff with a fork and serve.

Father Martin's Pizza Dough

When Father Martin prepares to throw his very famous pizza party, the Priory cafeteria turns into a veritable pizzeria. Whether the farina flies all over, no one knows, but the results after kneading a prezioso three pound mass of dough are molto amàbile è delizioso!

Father Martin

Makes 12 pizzas

3 pounds high gluten bread flour
3 quarts water
½ cup active dry yeast
3 tablespoons sugar
1 cup olive oil
3 tablespoons sea salt

Mix 1 quart warm water with the sugar and yeast and let it ferment for about 5 minutes, until it starts to bubble. Add the remaining water, salt and olive oil; mix well. Add the flour into a large bowl, add water mixture and mix until a dough is formed. Knead until smooth. Let dough sit for about an hour, covered, in a warm place.

Punch dough down and let it sit and rise for another hour or so before punching it down again. Then, do as Father Martin says: "Throw it into the refrigerator."

It is best to make the dough one or two days before using it, but take it out of the refrigerator at least an hour before preparing to bring to room temperature. Knead the dough into pizza-sized balls and let them sit for about fifteen minutes. This will make the dough more manageable for rolling. Roll each dough into the desired rounds, cover with toppings and bake in a 450- to 500-degree oven until done, about 5 minutes.

It is Father Martin's philosophy to be light on the toppings to let the true pizza flavor show through. Have fun!

Mary Lou's Polenta Lasagna

Kent Putnam's mother, Mary Lou, offers an interesting spin on traditional lasagna, using polenta layers instead of pasta. Not a fan of pasta, she created this Italian-inspired recipe as a means to marry her meat sauce with spinach and ricotta cheese. This dish can be made strictly vegetarian by replacing the meat with grilled eggplant or zucchini. We even liked the idea of keeping the meat and adding the grilled vegetables—like any normal lasagna, it's very versatile.

Trixie Putnam
Matthew 2011
Kent, graduated 8th grade in 1978

Serves 6

Polenta

2 teaspoons salt
1 cup dry polenta
¾ cup Parmesan or Romano cheese, divided

Sauce

1 pound ground chuck or Italian sausage, casings removed
2 tablespoons olive oil, plus additional for cooking meat if needed
1 cup chopped onion
2 cloves garlic, minced
1 (7½ ounce can) diced tomatoes
1 (8 ounce can) tomato sauce
1 (6 ounce can) tomato paste
2 teaspoons dried basil
1 teaspoon dried oregano
Salt and pepper

Filling

1 egg, beaten
15-ounce carton ricotta cheese
10-ounce package frozen spinach, thawed and drained
3 tablespoons chopped parsley
6 ounces mozzarella, shredded
Breadcrumbs for the top, about ¼ cup

Preheat oven to 375 degrees. Prepare two 8 by 8-inch pans with butter or cooking spray.

Polenta: Bring 4½ cups of water to a boil in a heavy saucepan and add the 2 teaspoons of salt. Remove water from heat source and whisk in the polenta to avoid clumping. Bring the polenta back to a slow simmer and cook, stirring frequently, until thick, about 30 minutes. Add ½ cup of cheese and stir well. Divide polenta equally between the two pans and smooth to approximately ¼-inch thick. Set aside.

Sauce: Brown the meat over medium-high heat in a large sauté pan, breaking it up with the back of your spoon until the pink is gone, and adding olive oil if needed. Drain fat and remove to separate dish. In the same pan, add the oil and cook the onions and garlic on medium heat until soft, about 5 minutes. Stir in un-drained tomatoes, tomato sauce, tomato paste, basil, oregano and salt and pepper to taste. Add reserved meat to tomato mixture and cook for 20 minutes to combine flavors.

Filling: Combine the egg, ricotta, spinach, remaining ¼ cup of Parmesan or Romano cheese, parsley and mozzarella cheese.

Place one half of the sauce directly on top of the polenta in one pan, and then spread out one half of the cheese filling over the sauce. Remove the second polenta layer from the other pan and place over the first sauce and cheese layer; press to evenly distribute. Top with the remaining sauce, then

(continued)

261

cheese mixture and top with the breadcrumbs.

Bake in the preheated oven for 30 to 35 minutes until melted and bubbly. Let stand for 5 minutes before serving. Cut into serving-sized pieces and use a spatula to plate.

Tester's Comments: *I cannot wait to make this for my mother the next times she visits. She will love to learn how to make such a delicious, unusual one-dish meal.*

Susan Ahlstrom

~∂~

Side Dishes

Weekly Chapel

Every Tuesday morning the entire Priory community gathers in the chapel. It is a time for prayer and song, announcements and reflection. Weekly Chapel is an opportunity to reflect on world events or to celebrate individual achievements as a community. Often a teacher or a student gives a talk about an event or experience that has had special meaning to them. Weekly Chapel is the spiritual heart of the school week.

For the Thanksgiving chapel in 1998, students planned a service not only to give thanks, but also to celebrate the international nature of the Priory community. Students from various ethnic traditions presented traditional breads, gave thanks for their heritage, and asked blessings for all people who are less fortunate. We reprint their words below:

Pan Mexicana is brought to this table today. It symbolizes our Latin American neighbors and their rich heritage. May it satisfy all who seek relief from war, hurricane damage, and famine.

Challah is brought to the table today. May it call to mind the celebration of peace. Let us remember all who, like the Jewish people, have had to flee their homelands in search of peace.

Sourdough Bread is brought to the table today. As a sign of our local tradition, it has as its leavening agent a small amount of dough kept from its last batch. May it be for us a sign that each of us must be an agent in the cause of freedom and justice.

Rice cakes are brought to the table today. Rice is a staple of many Asian cultures. In ancient Asia rice was rare and treasured, and used for medicinal purposes. May it heal the minds and bodies of those who are sick.

Cornbread is brought to the table today. May corn represent the indigenous cultures of the Americas and call to mind the First Thanksgiving. May it remind us of all races and cultures who have been oppressed by unjust structures.

Pita is brought to the table today. Let us remember our neighbors in the Middle East who are seeking peace and reconciliation among nations.

Russian Pumpernickel Bread is brought to the table today. May it represent all of our thanksgiving for the end of the Cold War conflict and our collective commitment to living peacefully on the Earth. May it satisfy the hunger of all who work for peace.

Scalloped Potatoes
with Fennel and Onions

Do not let the licorice taste of fennel turn you away from this recipe. The fennel mellows in flavor as it sautés in the butter with the onions, and then cooks in the light Béchamel sauce with the potatoes. Adding the rich Emmenthaler cheese to the mix creates a dish worthy of your most important guests.

Martha Luemers
Robert 2008

Serves 8

2 pounds low-starch potatoes such as red, Yellow Finnish or Yukon Gold
1 tablespoon olive oil
1 tablespoon butter
2 medium large sweet onions, cut into wedges and thinly sliced
2 large fennel bulbs, cut into quarters, cored and thinly sliced
3 tablespoons flour
3 cups of milk, heated
2 cups coarsely grated Emmenthaler cheese, divided
1 teaspoon salt or to taste
1 teaspoon freshly ground rainbow peppercorns
¾ teaspoon freshly grated nutmeg, or to taste

Preheat oven to 350 degrees.

Place whole, unpeeled potatoes in a saucepan and cover with water. Salt the water and bring to a boil over medium heat. Simmer gently until cooked but still firm, about 10 to 15 minutes, depending on the size of the potatoes. Drain and place in an ice bath if desired. When potatoes are cooled, peel and slice in ¼-inch rounds. Set aside.

Heat the olive oil and butter in a large sauté pan over medium heat. Add onions and fennel, cook until onions are limp. Sprinkle the vegetables with the flour and cook, stirring constantly, for 2 minutes.

Gradually add the hot milk one cup at a time to the onion fennel mixture until it boils and thickens. Be sure to add the second and finally the third cup only after bringing the previous addition of milk to a boil. Add 1½ cups of cheese and cook over medium-low heat until melted. Add salt to taste with the pepper and nutmeg and stir to distribute.

Cover the bottom of a 13 x 9-inch baking dish with one half of the potatoes, overlapping them as needed. Cover the potatoes with one half of the onion/fennel mixture. Repeat with the rest of the potatoes and then place the remaining onion/fennel mixture over the potatoes. Top with the remaining ½ cup of cheese. The dish can be refrigerated at this point, but make sure to bring it to room temperature before baking.

Bake for 30 minute and let stand for 10 minutes before cutting and serving.

Provençal Au Gratin Potatoes

The mix of creamy potatoes beneath the velvety cheese topping turns this classic potato dish into an updated favorite. While you may be tempted to use a food processor to slice the potatoes and grate the cheese, don't. The potatoes come out too thin for proper cooking and Gruyere is a cooking cheese which melts quickly in the cream if crumbled. These potatoes are a must side dish when serving Roasted Whole Fillet Mignon with a Port Wine Sauce (page 200).

Bengta Baker-Aboud
Daniel 2008

Serves 8

2 cups heavy cream
5 ounces Gruyère cheese, grated
8 to 10 large Yukon Gold potatoes, peeled and thinly sliced
Salt and pepper to taste

Preheat oven to 350 degrees. Butter the bottom and sides of a 12 x 9-inch baking dish.

Heat the cream and Gruyère cheese on low until the cheese has melted. Layer the potatoes and the cream mixture in the baking dish, starting with potatoes and ending with the cheese/cream mixture on top. Gently press down on each layer to evenly distribute cream. Salt and pepper each layer.

Bake in preheated oven for 1 hour. Let set for 10 minutes before cutting and serving.

Garlic Roasted Potatoes

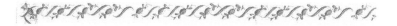

Taken from Ina Garten's *The Barefoot Contessa* cookbook, this dish should be in everyone's recipe repertoire. Begin the browning process by placing your roasting pan in the oven to heat. Coat the pan with cooking spray then place the potatoes cut side down on the hot pan. This ensures you will get nicely browned potatoes.

Lisa Plain
Hap 2006
Alexandra 2008

Serves 8

3 pounds small red potatoes, washed and well dried
¼ cup olive oil
1½ teaspoon kosher salt
1 teaspoon black pepper
2 tablespoons minced garlic (about 6 cloves)
2 tablespoons minced fresh parsley
Salt to taste

Preheat oven to 400 degrees. Place roasting pan in oven to heat.

Cut potatoes in half, place in a mixing bowl and toss with olive oil, salt, pepper and garlic until well coated. Spread in a single layer, cut side down, on a hot roasting pan sprayed with vegetable spray. Roast for 45 minutes, until brown and crisp. Flip once while baking. Remove the potatoes from oven and toss with parsley. Season to taste with additional salt if needed.

Serve hot.

Corn Pudding

Lisa Plain received this tasty recipe from her father, Kenneth Hall. This is an excellent dish to bring to a potluck or to serve when feeding a large group, because it is simple to prepare, easily doubled and is liked by everyone.

Lisa Plain
Hap 2006
Alex 2008

Serves 8

1 (12 ounce can) evaporated milk
3 eggs
1 tablespoon sugar
1 teaspoon vanilla
1 ½ teaspoon salt
1 teaspoon nutmeg
2 tablespoons cornstarch
1 (14 ounce can) whole corn, drained
1 (14 ounce can) creamed corn
2 tablespoons butter, melted

Preheat over to 350 degrees. Grease a 9 x 13-inch dish.

Combine evaporated milk, eggs, sugar, vanilla, salt, nutmeg and cornstarch in a large mixing bowl. Beat until fluffy. Add whole corn, creamed corn and melted butter. Stir well. Pour into prepared dish, stirring once before placing in oven.

Bake for 45 minutes, until slightly browned and a knife inserted into middle comes out clean. Please note: it will still be a little jiggly.

೫

Creamy Corn Confetti

This rich side dish from *Southern Living* is not for dieters but it is a true treat. Vary the look of the final presentation by using yellow and orange bell peppers along with the red and green, or spice it up a bit by adding a minced Serrano pepper.

Lisa Plain
Hap 2006
Alex 2008

Serves 10

8 slices of bacon, chopped
4 cups freshly cut corn kernels, about 6 ears
1 medium onion, chopped
⅓ cup chopped red bell pepper
⅓ cup chopped green bell pepper
8-ounce package cream cheese, cubed (easier to cube if chilled or slightly frozen)
½ cup half & half
1 teaspoon sugar
1 teaspoon salt
1 teaspoon pepper

Cook bacon in a large skillet until crisp. Remove bacon from pan; drain on paper towels, set aside. Reserve 2 tablespoons rendered bacon fat in skillet. Sauté onion, red and green peppers in reserved fat for approximately 2 minutes just until they are beginning to soften. Add corn and sauté for an additional 2 more minutes.

274

Lower the heat; add cream cheese and half & half, stirring until cream cheese is melted. Stir in sugar, salt, pepper and bacon.

Serve hot.

Tester's Comments: *I sautéed the onions, peppers and corn, then set it aside as I prepared the rest of my meal. When I was ready to serve, I added the cream cheese and half & half and heated it until the corn was hot and the cheese melted, about two minutes on medium. I added a bit more sugar since the corn was out of season, which helped make it taste like freshly picked summer corn.*

Sharon Traeger

Gulliver's Creamed Corn

For many years there was a chain of English-style restaurants named Gulliver's that served a creamed corn side dish so loved by the Conde family that they requested the recipe. The straightforward recipe can be easily doubled or tripled and refrigerates well for leftovers, making it an ideal dish to prepare during the holidays. For a smoother texture, purée half of the corn in a blender before combining with the other ingredients.

Tim Conde
Melanie 2011

Serves 6

10 ounces fresh or frozen (thawed) kernel corn (about 4 cups)
½ cup whipping cream
½ cup whole milk
½ teaspoon salt
1 tablespoon sugar
Pinch white pepper
1 tablespoon butter, softened
1 tablespoon flour

Combine corn, cream, milk, salt, sugar and pepper in a pot and bring to a boil. Simmer 5 minutes. Blend butter and flour together in a separate bowl. Add to corn mixture, mix well and cook an additional 2 minutes. Remove from heat and allow to thicken slightly.

Marinated Grilled Vegetables

Sunset Magazine provides us, outdoor living folk, with an array of easy, yet flavorful, recipes for the grill. This recipe in particular makes a delicious grilled vegetable sublime with the addition of a tasty marinade. Vegetables, like meat, develop flavor when soaked in a salty, savory liquid. Using a vegetable basket to barbeque the mix is an easy alternative to the standard skewers.

Jean Young
Ryan 2012

Serves 8

8 cups mixed vegetables (such as broccoli, zucchini, yellow squash, green and red bell peppers, mushrooms or red or sweet onions) cut into 1½- to 2-inch pieces

Marinade

1 cup Worcestershire sauce
1 cup balsamic vinegar
1 cup soy sauce
1 cup olive oil

In a large bowl, add the Worcestershire sauce, balsamic vinegar and soy sauce; stir to combine. Whisk in oil. Add vegetables and marinate for at least 2 hours, stirring periodically.

Preheat barbeque to high.

Place vegetables in a barbeque basket and place on barbeque. Cook for 10 to 15 minutes, shaking and turning the basket frequently. Serve immediately.

Helsinki Vegetable Pie

Sue Lowe was pleasantly surprised when she found out that her first try at a recipe from *Gourmet* magazine was a complete success. She felt the recipe simply must have been infallible, but we think she had the taste to pick a great one. This dish is filled with healthy ingredients—carrots, celery, onions, brown rice and cabbage—but is made especially flavorful with rich Jarlsberg cheese and herbs, all deliciously contained within a crispy piecrust. Just open up a nice bottle of crisp white wine and enjoy.

Sue Lowe
Taylor Franklin 2002 - 2004
Alix Franklin 2010

Serves 8

7 tablespoons butter
2 cups shredded carrots
1 rib celery, chopped
½ cup sliced green onions
2 garlic cloves, minced
6 cups finely shredded cabbage
1 teaspoon salt
2 cups Jarlsberg cheese, shredded
1 ½ cups cooked brown rice
¼ cup minced fresh parsley
¼ cup minced mixed herbs (combination of thyme, tarragon, chervil, basil…)
¼ cup whipping cream
1 teaspoon salt
1 teaspoon dried oregano
Pinch of nutmeg

278

Pinch of allspice

2 premade, deep-dish piecrusts; 1 prebaked (see note) and one for the
  lattice crust

1 egg white

Preheat oven to 400 degrees.

Melt butter in a sauté pan over medium heat; sauté the carrots, celery, green
onions and garlic for about five minutes. Add cabbage and salt; cook, stirring
periodically, for another ten minutes or until the cabbage is cooked through.
Set aside. Mix the Jarlsberg cheese, brown rice, parsley, whipping cream, salt,
oregano, nutmeg and allspice in a bowl. Add the cooked vegetables and mix
together. Put the mixture in the prebaked piecrust. Roll out the other pastry
crust and cut to lattice on top of the vegetables and brush with egg white.
Cook for 45 minutes.

Recipe Note: To pre-bake a pie shell, cover the frozen crust in foil; place
either pie weights, dried beans or rice evenly over the foil and place in a
preheated 350-degree oven for 15 minutes. Remove the weights and foil
and return crust to the oven for an additional 5 minutes. Pre-baking will
create a crispier crust.

Whipped Sweet Potatoes
with Pecan Streusel

Here is another wonderful holiday side dish from Lisa Plain. She received this recipe from her friend, Nancy Closs, three years ago and it has been a part of her Thanksgiving dinner ever since. The creaminess of the puréed sweet potatoes and the crunch of the topping is a winning combination. To create this dish in half the time, use canned sweet potatoes; the taste will not be compromised.

Lisa Plain
Hap 2006
Alex 2008

Serves 10

Potatoes

22 ounces sweet potatoes, peeled and cut into 1-inch cubes
6 tablespoons butter
1 egg
6 tablespoons sugar
1 teaspoon pumpkin pie spice
Salt to taste

Topping

1½ cups crushed cornflakes
½ cup brown sugar
½ cup chopped pecans
6 tablespoons butter, melted

Preheat oven to 400 degrees. Prepare a 9 x 9-inch pan with butter.

Place sweet potatoes in a stockpot and cover with water. Bring to a boil and cook until tender, about 15 minutes. Drain, place in a large bowl, add butter and beat with a hand-held mixer until smooth. Add egg, sugar, pumpkin pie spice and salt to taste. Beat again until well combined. Pour into prepared pan. May be made ahead of time up to this point, but bring to room temperature before baking. Bake for 25 minutes.

While baking, place cornflakes, brown sugar, pecans and butter in a small bowl, mixing well and breaking the cornflakes slightly. Spoon over hot potatoes. Bake 10 more minutes. Serve immediately.

Roasted Asparagus
with Balsamic Browned Butter

This simple but distinctive dish is perfect for a crowd. Have the sauce prepared before your guests arrive and the asparagus ready to pop in the oven at the last minute. Toss the cooked asparagus with the sauce and your side dish is good to go.

Betsy Haehl
Alicia Kriewall 2007

Serves 6 to 8

40 asparagus spears (about 2 pounds), trimmed
Olive oil for coating
¼ teaspoon kosher salt
⅛ teaspoon black pepper
4 tablespoons butter
4 teaspoons low-sodium soy sauce
1 tablespoon balsamic vinegar

Preheat oven to 400 degrees.

Arrange asparagus in a single layer on a baking sheet. Sprinkle with olive oil, salt and pepper. Toss to coat. Bake for 12 minutes or until tender.

Melt the butter in a small skillet over medium heat; cook for 3 minutes or until lightly browned, shaking pan occasionally. Cooking the butter until it browns will give the dish a nutty flavor but watch carefully, it can burn easily. Remove from heat; stir in soy sauce and vinegar. Drizzle roasted asparagus with the butter mixture, tossing well to coat. Serve immediately.

Sweet and Sour Broccoli

Try this cool, tangy sweet side dish in the summer, when the thought of boiling a pot of water brings on hot flashes. Crunchy broccoli is paired with raisins in a creamy, easy-to-make dressing. Lisa's sister-in-law, Kelly Hall, was gracious enough to share her recipe with us.

Lisa Plain
Hap 2006
Alex 2008

Serves 6

¼ cup sugar
¾ cup mayonnaise
2 tablespoons apple cider vinegar
4 cups raw broccoli, about two large heads, cut into bite-sized portions
¼ cup raisins
8 slices bacon, cooked and crumbled
¼ cup chopped red or sweet yellow onion

Combine sugar, mayonnaise and vinegar; whisk until smooth. Place broccoli, raisins, bacon and onion in a serving bowl; add dressing and toss. Chill for at least two hours before serving.

May be prepared a day in advance.

Tester's Comments: *I wasn't sure I would enjoy a side dish made of raw broccoli, but after the flavors were left to develop I loved the sweet-tart flavor of the crunchy broccoli. I cut the broccoli into small pieces and made sure the salad was cold before serving. It is a perfect summer side dish.*

Ann Dingerson and the Corkery Family

Microwave Cranberry-Apple Relish

Are you looking for a quick and easy, yet delicious, cranberry sauce recipe for your next holiday dinner spread? Lisa Plain was kind enough to offer hers, which is special enough to be placed in your best crystal bowl next to the star attraction, your roasted turkey. While this recipe is made for the microwave, you can just as easily place all the ingredients in a saucepan and cook for the appropriate 12 to 15 minutes.

Lisa Plain
Hap 2006
Alexandra 2008

Serves 10

1 cup sugar
¼ teaspoon ground cloves
¼ teaspoon allspice
¼ teaspoon cinnamon
½ cup apple juice
1 pound fresh cranberries (4 cups)
2 medium unpeeled apples, coarsely chopped
½ cup chopped nuts (preferably walnuts or pecans)

Mix together sugar, cloves, allspice, cinnamon and apple juice in a 2-quart microwave-safe dish. Stir in cranberries and apples. Cover loosely with waxed paper. Microwave on high for 8 to10 minutes, stirring half way through. Uncover and microwave on high for 4 more minutes. Stir in nuts. Cool before serving.

This dish is better served on the second day; the flavors are more developed and the color is brighter.

⁓

Tester's Comments: *Lisa suggested using a blush apple such as Fuji, Pink Lady or Braeburn. At the time of year I tested this recipe, there were no fresh cranberries so I used frozen ones with excellent results. My son, who doesn't like anything, had to admit it was pretty darn good! This is my new cranberry sauce recipe for our holiday dinners.*

Patty Turnquist

Desserts

A Family Kitchen

Boarding school food—these three words bring to mind grim trays laden with gray slices of mystery meat accompanied by watery piles of earth-toned glop. Not so at Woodside Priory School, however! From the very beginning, the dining hall at the Priory has served students, faculty and members of the monastic community meals prepared with love by women and men who cooked as if for their own families.

Father Egon chose Father Leopold to be in charge of the first kitchen. Father Egon reasoned that because Father Leopold had a doctorate in biology he would best be able to determine what was poisonous and what was not! The dining hall that exists today opened in 1964, and Father Maurus took over cafeteria operations in 1971. Kay Falk, mother-in-law of current registrar Barbara Falk, and Estelle Spears, mother of current cook Nate Spears, were the cooks and Jesse Paton was the manager. They prepared the meals in the old manner, without recipes and through their own personal experience and culinary tastes. Both Mrs. Falk and Mrs. Spears were experienced bakers and made fabulous desserts and cakes from scratch. Even though Father Maurus admonished the staff to adhere to modest portions both for dietary and monetary reasons, Mrs. Spears could not resist her maternal urge to give the boys generous servings. Students were required to finish everything on their plates, especially vegetables, if they wanted second helpings! Nate Spears began accompanying his mother to the Priory when he was a little boy. He joined the kitchen staff five years before his mother retired in 1986 and now boasts of twenty-five years of employment at the Priory.

Peter Agoston became head chef and kitchen manager in 1990. Of American-Hungarian descent, he began his culinary career in Hungary as an apprentice in restaurant kitchens. Peter proudly continues the Priory tradition of home-cooked meals. For example, he prepares foods from many countries not only because of the internationally diverse student body, but also because he feels that exposure to different cuisines is part of the students' education. He also believes that the school dining hall is a natural place to help Priory students develop a taste for healthy foods. An organic salad bar is now part of every lunch and dinner, and homemade salad dressings entice those students who may still be wary of eating something green. Indeed, when Priory students think of boarding school food, it is quite possible that coconut-lime cilantro salad dressing springs to mind!

Kuchelhof

Alix Franklin is a pro at making her Austrian grandmother's delicious, soul-comforting cake. It is tasty alone, but the addition of berries, ice cream or chocolate sauce is what truly makes this dessert special. We thought it was best with all three!

Sue Lowe
Taylor Franklin 2002 graduated 8th grade
Alix Franklin 2010

Serves 8

2 tablespoons bread crumbs
1½ cups sugar
1 teaspoon vanilla
1 (16 ounce) container of sour cream
2 cups self-rising flour
4 eggs

Preheat oven to 350 degrees. Prepare a bundt pan with cooking spray and sprinkle it with breadcrumbs.

Combine sugar, vanilla and sour cream in a food processor and process until blended. Add the eggs one at a time, and incorporate completely before adding the next. Add the flour to the processor in three batches and pulse to blend in. Pour batter into pan and bake for 45 minutes or until a toothpick placed in the center comes out clean.

Tester's Comments: *This recipe took less than 5 minutes to make, and left very little clean up (I just put the food processor in the dishwasher). I served it with strawberries and whipped cream but it would be just as delicious on its own with a cup of tea.*

Susan Dennis

Chocolate Decadence

It was 1983 and the famous Berkeley chef and entrepreneur Narsai David was on KCBS "Kitchen Talk." His luscious description of a decadent chocolate cake prompted Margaret Herzen to write to the station for the recipe. Here it is now for all of you chocolate lovers to enjoy nearly 25 years later...

Margaret Herzen
Elena 2003
Juliana 2007

Serves 8 to 10

Butter and flour for preparing pan
1 pound of good quality bittersweet chocolate, cut into small pieces
5 ounces unsalted butter
4 whole eggs
1 tablespoon sugar
1 tablespoon flour

Preheat oven to 425 degrees.

Butter and flour an 8-inch springform pan. Place a circle of parchment paper at the bottom of the pan.

Melt chocolate with butter in a double boiler, or in your microwave, until just melted. Set aside.

Beat whole eggs and sugar in a double boiler until sugar dissolves and mixture is lukewarm (do not overcook). Remove from heat and whip until volume has at least quadrupled and is thick. Fold flour into eggs. Stir ¼ egg mixture into chocolate, then fold chocolate into egg mixture. Pour into the prepared springform pan and bake for no longer than 15 minutes (cake will be liquid in center). Freeze, preferably overnight, before removing from pan. Carefully dip bottom of pan into hot water to unmold. Mask with whipped cream and decorate with shaved chocolate. Refrigerate until serving. Serve with raspberry purée strained through a sieve to remove seeds.

❧

Tester's Comments: *This is a very rich, versatile dessert. You can use whipped cream and raspberry sauce as recommended, or vanilla ice cream with any fruit topping. After I baked the cake, I left it to cool. When I returned a few hours later, there was a HUGE wedge missing! So perhaps it's best to make two—one for dessert and one for those who wander through the kitchen and can't resist the chocolate decadence!*

Georgia Baba

Kahlúa Chocolate Bundt Cake

While this recipe calls for a cake mix as its base, the addition of Kahlúa, sour cream and chocolate chips transforms this dessert into a decadent cake that will leave no one the wiser. The moist, chocolaty cake looks beautiful with a sprinkling of powdered sugar and a few raspberries. To make it a truly special treat for your guests, pass around a pitcher of Maggie's Magic Chocolate Sauce (page 317) to pour over the top.

Roberta Harryman
Will 2007
Ryan 2009

Serves 8

1 package devil's food cake mix
1 cup Kahlúa
¾ cup oil
4 eggs
1 cup sour cream
1 cup mini chocolate chips
Powdered sugar and raspberries for garnish

Preheat oven to 350 degrees. Grease and flour a Bundt pan.

Add the cake mix into the bowl of your mixer. In a 4-cup measuring bowl, mix Kahlúa, oil, eggs and sour cream, blending well. With the mixer on medium speed, slowly add the Kahlúa mixture to the cake mix and beat until just combined. Fold in chocolate chips and then pour into prepared bundt pan.

Bake for 50 minutes or until a toothpick inserted in the center comes out

294

clean. Let cool. Invert onto cake plate and remove bundt pan. Garnish with powdered sugar and raspberries.

❧

Tester's Comments: *Every single one of my guests I served this cake to had seconds!*

Emily Goldberg

Almond Cake

While Kelly Pettit serves this cake as part of a brunch buffet, we think it is rich enough to be a perfect finish to a great dinner. Just place the batter in an ungreased, 8-inch cake pan and serve with whipped cream and a few berries. This cake is a must for almond lovers.

Kelly Pettit
Angela 2008

Makes 15 1½-inch squares

1 cup (two sticks) salted butter
¾ cup sugar
1 egg, separated
½ cup (4 ounces) almond paste (not almond filling)
1 teaspoon almond extract
2 cup sifted all-purpose flour
¼ cup sliced almonds

Preheat oven to 350 degrees. Have an ungreased, 8-inch square pan ready.

In large bowl beat butter and sugar with an electric mixer at medium speed until light and fluffy. Beat yolk into butter mixture. Add almond extract and almond paste and beat until almond paste has incorporated into the batter and is smooth. With mixture at low speed, beat in flour just until combined.

Press mixture into pan and smooth the top; set aside. Beat egg white until frothy, then brush over top of batter. Cover with sliced almonds.

Bake 30 minutes or until golden brown. Cool completely on wire rack, then cut into 1½-inch squares.

Best Carrot Cake In History!

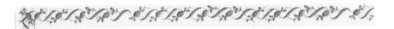

Tim Conde's family loves carrot cake, so he went out of his way to create the absolute best. This recipe, which he has perfected, gives the cake just the right balance between moisture and taste. The ratio of flour to the other ingredients is low, so be prepared for a loose batter.

Tim Conde
Melanie 2012

Serves 6

Cake

2 cups sugar
1½ cups vegetable oil
4 eggs
2 cups all-purpose flour, sifted
2 teaspoons baking soda
1 teaspoon salt
2 teaspoons cinnamon
1 (8 ounce can) crushed pineapple, drained
1 cup chopped walnuts
1 teaspoon vanilla
2 cups grated carrots

Cream Cheese Frosting

1 (1 pound box) powdered sugar
1 (8 ounce package) cream cheese
1 teaspoon vanilla
½ cup unsalted butter, room temperature
Milk or cream

Preheat the oven to 350 degrees. Grease and flour three 8-inch round cake pans.

Beat the sugar, oil and eggs together in a mixing bowl. In a separate bowl, combine the flour, baking soda, salt and cinnamon, and add into the wet ingredients until well combined. Stir in the pineapple, walnuts, vanilla and carrots until well blended. Distribute the batter evenly in your pan or pans, and bake for 35 to 40 minutes. You may also use a greased and floured 9 x 13-inch pan but increase the baking time by 5 to 10 minutes.

While cake is cooking, make the frosting by mixing together sugar, cream cheese, vanilla and butter until smooth. Add a few teaspoons of milk or cream to get the desired consistency for spreading.

When cake is completely cooled, frost with cream cheese frosting.

Carrot Snack Cake

This recipe makes a great, healthy dessert. Since it's a lower calerie version with less sugar, this recipe benefits from the addition of raisins, walnuts or other yummy ingredient of your choice to add natural sweetness and flavor. It is best served warm.

Susan Light
Tim Kovachy 2005
Benny Kovachy 2010

Serves 8

2 eggs
½ cup frozen white grape juice concentrate
3 tablespoons vegetable oil or softened butter
¼ cup non-fat vanilla yogurt
1½ cups shredded carrot (may use pre-packaged carrots)
¼ cup chopped walnuts (optional)
¼ cup raisins (optional)
1¼ cups white whole wheat flour (King Arthur brand) or sifted whole
    wheat flour
¼ cup wheat germ
2 tablespoons granulated sugar
1 teaspoon cinnamon
½ teaspoon ginger
1 teaspoon baking soda
1 teaspoon baking powder

Preheat oven to 350 degrees. Prepare an 8 x 8-inch glass pan with cooking spray.

Blend together the eggs, grape juice concentrate, oil, yogurt and carrots in a large bowl. Mix in walnuts and raisins or other optional ingredients if using.

In another bowl, combine the flour, wheat germ, sugar, cinnamon, ginger, baking soda and baking powder.

Add the flour mixture to the egg mixture and blend, only enough to combine. Pour into prepared pan. Bake 30 to 35 minutes.

Tester's Comments: *I preferred this recipe served cool rather than warm as recommended. I would definitely use the raisins and walnuts for that added flavor but next time would also add a bit of crushed pineapple.*

Amy Magnuson

Banana Cake

When you have bananas on hand that are too ripe to eat but a waste to throw out, check out these next two recipes! The first is your classic banana bread version, which Jane Bessin claims to be the best banana cake ever. We tend to agree! She has been making it since her college days and it is moist and full of flavor, but not a dessert for the dieter. The second recipe is a lighter version with healthy oats thrown in for good measure. Both are quick and easy to put together and your family will be happy you did.

Jane Bessin
Julie 2007
David 2010

Serves 10

½ cup butter, softened
1¼ cups sugar
2 eggs slightly beaten
1 teaspoon baking soda
¼ cup sour cream (or plain, whole milk yogurt)
1 teaspoon vanilla
¼ teaspoon salt
1½ cups flour
1 cup mashed banana pulp (about 2 to 3 ripe bananas)

Preheat oven to 350 degrees. Prepare a loaf pan or 9-inch springform pan with butter or cooking spray.

Cream together butter and sugar; add eggs and beat well. Mix baking soda into sour cream to dissolve and add to butter mixture. Stir in vanilla.

Mix together salt and flour; add into butter mixture. Fold in bananas until completely incorporated. Pour into prepared pan. Bake for 45 minutes (in convection oven) or up to 1 hour in a standard oven or until toothpick placed into center of cake comes out clean. The springform pan will cook in about 45 minutes so check at 40.

꒐

Tester's Comments: *To me, bananas and chocolate go hand in hand. Accordingly, I heated up 1/3 cup of cream in a small saucepan and added 1½ cups of chocolate chips. Stir until melted and spread onto the cooled cake for a quick frosting. A true winner!*

Virginia Taylor

Banana Oatmeal Bread

This recipe for classic banana bread, from *Cooking Light* magazine, has been tweaked for today's tastes. It's great as an after school snack, or even served warm as a low calorie dessert, a la mode, with vanilla or chocolate non-fat frozen yogurt.

Irina Sarkisov
Katya 2006

Serves 12

1½ cups all-purpose flour
⅔ cup sugar
1½ teaspoons baking powder
¼ teaspoon salt
¾ cup old-fashioned natural rolled oats
1 cup mashed ripe bananas (about 2 to 3 ripe bananas)
⅓ cup low-fat buttermilk
¼ cup vegetable oil
1 teaspoon vanilla extract
2 large eggs, lightly beaten
Cooking spray

Preheat oven to 350 degrees. Prepare a 8 x 4-inch loaf pan with cooking spray.

Lightly spoon flour into dry measuring cups; level with a the flat edge of a knife. Combine flour, sugar, baking powder and salt in a large bowl, mixing well with a whisk. Stir in oats.

In a separate bowl, combine mashed banana, buttermilk, oil, vanilla extract and eggs. Add to the flour mixture. Stir just until moist. Spoon batter into prepared pan.

Bake for 55 minutes or until a wooden pick inserted into the center comes out clean. Cool 15 minutes in pan on a wire rack. Remove from pan and cool completely on a wire rack.

Apple Cake

When you are craving a fruit dessert in the winter, when no stone fruits are readily available, use this recipe. Add a ½ cup of raisins if you like that apple-walnut-raisin combination. The brown sugar frosting is quick to put together and adds the perfect amount of sweetness to the light cake.

Lisa Plain
Alex 2008
Hap 2006

Serves 12

1½ cups flour
½ teaspoon salt
1 teaspoon cinnamon
1 teaspoon nutmeg
1 teaspoon baking soda
½ cup shortening
1½ cups sugar
2 eggs
1 teaspoon vanilla
3 cups peeled, diced apples
½ cup chopped walnuts or pecans

Preheat oven to 350 degrees. Grease a 9 x 13-inch pan.

Combine flour, salt, cinnamon, nutmeg and soda in a medium bowl. Cream together the shortening, sugar, eggs and vanilla. Add flour mixture to the egg mixture in small portions until blended. Add the apples and nuts, blending well. Bake in the prepared pan for 30 minutes.

Icing

1½ cups packed brown sugar
2 tablespoons milk
3 tablespoons butter

While cake is cooking, combine brown sugar, milk and butter in a saucepan over low heat. Cook gently until smooth and remove from heat. Remove cake from oven after 30 minutes, pour icing over cake and return to oven, baking for another 20 minutes.

Let cool and serve warm or at room temperature.

Right Side Up Fruit Torte

Depending on the season, experiment with your fruits for this cake. Use a mixture of apples and blueberries or peaches and raspberries, or choose a single fruit like pears, apricots or plums. After the fruit is prepared, the batter can be put together in a snap with the use of a food processor.

Betsy Haehl
Alicia Kriewall 2007

Serves 10

2 tablespoons sugar (3 if using apricots or plums)
2 teaspoons cinnamon
3 cups fruit
½ cup (1 stick) salted butter
1 cup sugar
1 teaspoon vanilla extract
2 eggs
1 cup flour
1 teaspoon baking powder

Preheat oven to 350 degrees. Prepare a 9-inch springform pan with removable bottom with butter or vegetable spray.

Mix together the sugar and cinnamon and divide in half. If using pears, apples or peaches, peel, core or seed and thinly slice. No need to peel apricots or plums, just remove the seed and slice thinly.

Cream butter, sugar and vanilla in a food processor until combined well. Add eggs and continue processing until completely combined. Pulse in the flour and baking powder until thoroughly mixed.

Pour batter into prepared pan, smoothing the mixture so it is evenly distributed. Toss together fruit and one half of the cinnamon/sugar mixture. Lay the fruit on top of the batter. Sprinkle with the remaining cinnamon/sugar mixture. Bake for 50 to 60 minutes depending on the fruit, allowing less time for apples or pears, and more time if using peaches, apricots or plums.

Tester's Comments: *This versatile recipe adapts to any season and anytime of the day. I made it for dessert but loved it with my coffee the next morning.*

Cindy Shove

Creeping Cherry Cobbler

Jeff Purvin's mother, Frances, used to make this dessert for him when he was a young boy in Dallas. He was always amazed that the crust started out on the bottom (buried completely by cherry liquid) then, as the cobbler baked in the oven, the crust crept up through the liquid and ended up on the top! The true magic to this dessert, however, is that it takes less than 10 minutes to put together and it is absolutely delicious. No wonder Jeff carried around his mother's handwritten recipe for years!

Jeff Purvin
Colton 2011

Serves 8

¾ cup butter
1½ cups flour
⅛ teaspoon salt
3 cups sugar (divided)
1½ teaspoons baking powder
¾ cup milk
2 (14.5-ounce) cans pitted sour cherries, in water (only use sour cherries)
1 tablespoon fresh lemon juice

Preheat the oven to 375 degrees.

Prepare a 12 x 9-inch glass baking dish with vegetable spray.

Melt the butter and pour into the baking dish. Sift together the flour, salt, 1½ cups of sugar and baking powder in a separate mixing bowl. Add the milk and stir well.

In a separate saucepan, warm the cherries and their juice with the remaining sugar (only use 3/4 cup if using cherries in light syrup). Pour the milk/flour mixture into the baking dish over the melted butter. Do not stir. Pour the warmed cherries and their juice carefully over the batter. Do not stir. Sprinkle the lemon juice on top of the cherries.

Put the baking dish in the oven and bake until the batter creeps to the top and is evenly browned. This usually takes about 30 minutes.

Serve the cobbler fresh out of the oven in deep bowls, with a scoop of vanilla ice cream on top of each serving.

Berries with Stars

Martha Luemers and her neighbor have been working to perfect this recipe and we think they have. Their secret: a combination of berries that always starts with 2 cups of raspberries and 1 cup of blueberries plus their technique of baking the pastry topping separately from the fruit which creates a beautifully tasting dish without the crust becoming stained. Use a variety of cookie cutters depending on the season.

Martha Luemers
Robert 2008

Serves 4

Berries

2 cups raspberries (do not substitute strawberries)
2 cups blueberries (or substitute blackberries or boysenberries for one cup)
2 teaspoons fresh lemon juice
½ cup sugar
2 tablespoons flour

Stars

1 tablespoon sugar
2 tablespoons unsalted butter
¾ cup flour
¼ teaspoon salt
1½ teaspoons baking powder
⅓ cup whipping cream
Sugar for sprinkling

Preheat the oven to 400 degrees.

Toss berries with lemon juice in a large bowl. Combine the sugar and flour; sprinkle onto the berry mixture and toss until evenly distributed. Bake in a 1½-quart soufflé dish for 30 minutes.

In a food processor, pulse the sugar, butter, flour, salt and baking powder until well distributed. While processor is running, gradually add whipping cream. Form into a disc and refrigerate for at least 30 minutes.

Roll out dough to 3/8 inch thick and cut out stars with a cookie cutter. Place stars on parchment paper on a cookie sheet, sprinkle with sugar, and bake until very lightly browned, approximately 10 to 15 minutes.

Arrange stars on top of berries and serve warm but not hot. Berries and stars can be made in advance, left out at room temperature, then assembled and put in a warm oven during dinner.

Serve with vanilla ice cream.

Tester's Comments: *Recipe is easily doubled. To make this dessert in individual servings, divide berries after cooking into 4-inch ramekins and top with one star before serving (can be reheated in this form). This dessert is best served warm.*

Patty Turnquist

Low-Sugar Huckleberry Pie

You must use Wyman's Wild Blueberries (known as huckleberries in many parts of the country) canned in water—not fresh, frozen or standard canned blueberries—for this satisfying pie. You can find them at Whole Foods or any specialty grocery store. The pie filling is thickened with flour over the stove, so be sure to reduce the huckleberry water to the proper consistency before adding the huckleberries. The filling will still be quite loose and is excellent with this foolproof crust.

Courtesy of Virginia Valentine,
a friend of the Purvin Family
Colton 2011

Makes 2 pies

Filling

3 (14-ounce) cans Wyman's Wild Blueberries, packed in water
1½ cup Splenda sugar substitute
1 cup sugar
1 teaspoon cinnamon
1 teaspoon salt
6 tablespoons all-purpose flour
6 tablespoons butter

Crust

3 ½ cups all-purpose flour
1 teaspoon salt
1 teaspoon baking powder
1⅛ cups Crisco
½ cup, plus 2 tablespoons boiling water

1 egg white
Sugar for sprinkling on pie crust

Preheat oven to 375 degrees.

Drain blueberries, reserving juice. Handle the blueberries gently to avoid breaking them.

Combine the Splenda, sugar, cinnamon, salt and flour in a medium-sized saucepan; whisk to incorporate. Stir in the juice from the blueberries and cook over medium heat, stirring constantly until smooth and thick, about 10 minutes. Add butter and continue to stir until most of the butter has melted. Gently add the blueberries and stir until well combined. Set aside while preparing crust.

Mix the flour, salt and baking powder in a large bowl. Pour the boiling water into a separate bowl and add Crisco, cutting the Crisco with a fork until it has melted and fully mixed into the water. Pour the shortening water into the flour mixture. Mix everything completely and press down into the mixing bowl. Divide the dough into fourths. Allow the mixture to cool, but don't wait too long or it will get too cool and become crumbly. If this happens, heat it for 10 seconds in a microwave.

Roll each fourth of the pie dough between two sheets of waxed paper into a circle big enough for a 9-inch crust. Place one crust circle into each of the pie pans, pressing into pan. Set aside the other two.

Place half of the blueberry mixture into each of the prepared pie pans. Top each with a remaining circle of crust. Crimp the edges of the crusts together, and trim excess with a sharp knife or scissors. Brush the top of the pie with egg white and sprinkle with sugar. Cut steam holes.

Bake for about 30 to 40 minutes until lightly browned. Remove from oven.

Chill the pies before serving.

Cut the pies into six slices while cold, then (if desired) microwave them for 1½ minutes. Serve with a scoop of vanilla ice cream.

Georgia Pecan Pie

Have you forgotten how easy it is to make pecan pie? Well, with a good quality pie shell from the frozen aisle, a big handful of the best pecans you can find and five minutes of prep time, you can have a beauty ready to bake! And this pie is sure to cure anyone's sweet tooth.

Barbara Puckett and Kimily Conkle
Cade Conkle 2003-2006

Serves 8

½ cup sugar
1 cup light Karo syrup
1 teaspoon vanilla
½ teaspoon salt
3 eggs, slightly beaten
1 cup pecan halves
1 unbaked 9-inch pie shell

Preheat oven to 375 degrees.

In a large bowl combine the sugar, Karo syrup, vanilla, salt and eggs; mix well. Fold in pecans and pour into the unbaked pie crust. Bake in the lower half of the oven for 30 to 40 minutes. When center of pie is still slightly soft, pie is done. Do not over bake.

Ingredients Note: Two good sources for purchasing pecans are Sunnyland Farms (nutsandcandies.com ; 800-999-2488), and Pippin Snack Pecans (229-432-9316).

Maggie's Magic Chocolate Sauce

Once you make this chocolate sauce, you will never buy premade sauce again! The magic of this recipe is how the sauce blends into velvety syrup that is perfect on Kuckelhof (page 291), Banana Cake (page 302) or Kahlúa Chocolate Bundt Cake (page 294), but we also loved it simply on a scoop of vanilla ice cream.

Peggy Asprey
Susan 2005
Erik 2008

Serves 6

2 squares unsweetened Baker's chocolate
⅓ cup water
½ cup sugar
Few grains of salt

Heat chocolate and water in a small saucepan on medium heat, until melted (it will look dry). Add sugar, stirring well until it magically liquefies. Remove pan from heat and add few grains of salt.

Trifle Pudding

This dessert is a Christmas tradition in the Schofield home. Laurie makes the sponge cake a few days in advance and then cooks the custard and assembles the trifle on Christmas Eve. After she cleans up her Christmas Eve dishes, Laurie makes her trifle with the Pope, or so she says: The two final steps of this dessert take about as long as the midnight mass on TV! The amount of sherry you use depends on whether you like your trifle soaked with the fortified wine or with just a suggestion of it. Laurie's grandmother used so much sherry that the cake was flammable!

Laurie Schofield
Jack 2003
Will 2006

Serves 12

Sponge Cake

½ pound (2 sticks) unsalted butter, softened
1 cup sugar
4 eggs
2 teaspoons vanilla
2 cups flour
1 teaspoon baking powder

Custard

4 cups of milk
8 egg yolks
½ cup sugar
Dash salt
1 teaspoon vanilla
2 teaspoons almond extract

For assembling the pudding:

1 large jar seedless raspberry jam (32 ounces)
Dry sherry (not cream sherry)
2 cups (1 pint) whipping cream

Preheat oven to 350 degrees. Prepare two 8-inch square cake pans with butter or vegetable spray.

Cream butter and sugar until light in a standard or hand-held mixer. Beat in eggs, one at a time until incorporated, and then beat until light and fluffy, about 5 minutes. Add vanilla.

In a separate bowl, sift flour and baking powder. Fold flour gently into the butter/egg mixture. Divide the mixture between cake pans. Bake for about 20 minutes or until the cake springs back when lightly touched. The cakes will be golden in color (not browned) and will only be about 1 inch thick. You can make the cakes two or three days in advance, keeping them air tight in a Ziploc bag after they have cooled.

To make the custard, heat milk just before the boiling point. Beat egg yolks in the top of a double boiler over simmering water until warm. Stir in sugar and salt; mix. Gradually add milk. To avoid curdling the eggs, add a few tablespoons of the hot milk first and whisk to incorporate. Whisk in the remaining milk. Heat egg/milk mixture over simmering water, stirring constantly with a wooden spoon until the mixture is thick enough to coat the back of a spoon. It will be like a sauce, not a pudding. Watch and stir the custard constantly. This will take about 20 minutes. If you see bits of coagulated egg, take it off the heat immediately and whisk. Take the custard off the heat; add the vanilla and almond extract. The custard will thicken more as it cools.

To assemble the trifle, use a decorative deep dish approximately 12 x 8 x 3-inches. Cut the sponge cake into approximately 2-inch square pieces; the size and shape is not important. Line your serving dish with sponge cake,

(continued)

using one of the two cakes. It should fit tightly in one layer. Sprinkle with sherry to your taste. It can either be soaked (how Laurie's grandmother made it) or with just a suggestion of sherry. Spread the cake generously with half of the raspberry jam. Repeat with another layer of cake, sherry and the rest of the jam.

Take the entire amount of the still warm custard and begin to incorporate the liquid into the trifle. Start by pouring as much custard as will cover the cake and allowing it to sink in. To help sink the custard in, use a knife to create holes for the custard to escape. Keep pouring custard and making holes with your knife all over the pudding until the dish is full of custard soaked cake. The custard and jam will begin to incorporate and this is fine. Cover with plastic wrap and refrigerate overnight or at least 8 hours. A few hours before serving, whip the cream until fairly stiff, adding up to ¼ cup of sugar (if desired), and spread over the entire pudding.

Tester's Comments: *I like to make my trifles in a tall, somewhat narrow, glass dish, creating layers that can be seen through the glass. I started by placing half of the first sponge cake (¼ of the entire cake) in the bottom of my glass dish, covered it with jam, sprinkled it heavily with the sherry and covered that with the still warm custard. I continued, making three more layers, and ending with the custard. The next day I added the top layer of whipped cream and placed this beautiful creation on my dessert table.*

Virginia Taylor

Oatmeal Chocolate Chip Cookies

Interested in a whole wheat and grain cookie that is low in fat yet still tasty enough for your children to enjoy? Valerie Wookey developed this cookie with just such a snack in mind. To keep your cookies soft, store them in an airtight container with a piece of bread.

Valerie Wookey
Sarah 2010
Jack 2012

Makes 2 dozen

2 cups whole wheat flour
2 cups oatmeal
1 teaspoon baking soda
1 teaspoon baking powder
½ cup butter, softened
1 cup brown sugar
2 eggs
1 cup chocolate chips

Preheat oven to 350 degrees.

Mix together flour, oatmeal, baking soda and baking powder in a medium-sized bowl. Cream together butter and sugar in a standard mixer, hand mixer or wooden spoon in a large bowl. Add one egg, completely incorporating it before adding the next. Mix in flour mixture until just combined and then add chocolate chips. Drop rounded teaspoons of dough, 2 inches apart onto a cookie sheet. Bake for 12 to 15 minutes or until slightly browned.

Mexican Chocolate Cookies

These rich, dark chocolate cookies won the chocolate division of the dessert contest at Sue Young and her family's summer church camp in Redwood Glen a few years ago. Sue loves the combination of chocolate and spice. This recipe is from the chocolate master herself, Alice Medrich, who owned Cocolat, the acclaimed San Francisco chocolate and dessert store, years ago.

Sue Young
Andrew 2008
Al 2009

Makes 40 to 45

1 cup all-purpose flour
½ cup plus 1 tablespoon unsweetened Dutch Process cocoa
¼ teaspoon baking soda
¼ teaspoon salt
½ cup plus 1 tablespoon packed brown sugar
½ cup plus 1 tablespoons granulated sugar
3 tablespoons unsalted butter, slightly softened
3 tablespoons margarine
½ teaspoon ground cinnamon
Generous pinch of ground black pepper
Generous pinch of cayenne pepper
1 teaspoon vanilla
1 egg white

Preheat oven to 350 degrees.

Combine the flour, cocoa, soda and salt in a medium bowl. Mix thoroughly; set aside.

Combine the brown and granulated sugars in a small bowl and mix well, pressing out any lumps. (May use a food processor if lumps are stubborn).

In a medium-sized mixing bowl, cream the butter and margarine. Add sugar mixture, cinnamon, black and cayenne peppers, and vanilla. Beat on high speed for about one minute. Beat in egg white. Stop the mixer. Add the flour mixture. Beat on low speed just until incorporated. Gather the dough together with your hands and form it into a neat 9- to 10-inch log. Wrap in waxed paper. Fold or twist ends of paper without pinching or flattening the log. Chill at least 45 minutes, or until needed. For even easier slicing, it can be frozen. Place oven racks in the upper and lower third of the preheated oven. Line cookie sheet with parchment paper, aluminum foil or silpat.

Use a sharp knife to slice rounds of chilled dough a scant ¼ -inch thick. Place 1 inch apart on prepared baking sheets. Bake 12 to 14 minutes, rotating baking sheets from top to bottom and front to back about halfway through. Cookies will puff and crackle on top, and then will settle down slightly when done. Use a metal spatula to transfer cookies to a wire rack to cool. For easier removal, cool cookies only slightly, as the cookie becomes hard to remove as it cools. Allow cookies to cool completely on wire rack before storing or stacking. Cookies should be crisp. Store in an airtight container up to two weeks, or freeze up to 2 months.

Tester's Comments: *My daughter loved these cookies, as did my 94-year old "chocoholic" friend who could not wait to try them and, upon doing so, had only superlatives to describe them. The cookies are beautiful with crackled tops revealing rich chocolate beneath.*

Georgia Baba

Snickerdoodles

This classic cookie, which is Eric Frasch's (Class of 2007) favorite, is the one his mother grew up baking when she was a little girl. There's a reason it's such a tasty staple: the light, delicate cookie is made even sweeter with the coating of cinnamon and sugar. If it is not already one of your Christmas cookie favorites, it should be!

Linda Frasch
Lauren 2005
Eric 2007

Makes 6 dozen

½ cup butter or margarine, softened
½ cup shortening
1 ½ cups sugar
2 eggs
2 ¾ cups flour
2 teaspoons cream of tartar
1 teaspoon baking soda
¼ teaspoon salt

2 tablespoons sugar
2 teaspoons cinnamon

Preheat oven to 400 degrees.

Using a standard mixer, hand mixer or bowl and wooden spoon, thoroughly mix butter, shortening and sugar. Add the eggs one by one, blending well after each addition. In a small bowl, mix the flour, cream of tartar, baking soda and salt. Add flour mixture to butter/egg mixture and stir until just blended. Refrigerate for at least one hour to chill.

Place sugar and cinnamon in a small, shallow bowl and mix until incorporated. Shape rounded teaspoonfuls of dough into balls. Roll ball into sugar mixture. Place 2 inches apart on ungreased baking sheet. Bake 8 to 10 minutes or until set. Immediately remove from baking sheet onto cooling rack.

Tester's Comments: *The flavor is more intense when the cookies have cooled, so let them come to room temperature before serving. During the holidays, I will roll these cookies in colored sugar for a festive appearance. These are especially great cookies to bake during the holiday season since kids love to roll the dough and cover them in the cinnamon/sugar mixture.*

Emily Goldberg and Christie Bilikam

Tony's Oatmeal Lace Cookies

The recipe for these thin and fragile, yet divine, cookies comes from Betsy Haehl's grandmother-in-law. To keep the delicate cookies from breaking, Betsy cooks them on foil and lets them cool before removing. You can also use parchment paper or silpats with equal success.

Betsy Haehl
Alicia Kriewall 2007

Makes 3 dozen

1 cup quick-cooking oats
1 cup sugar
2 tablespoons flour
¼ teaspoon salt
¼ teaspoon baking powder
½ cup butter, melted
½ teaspoon vanilla
1 egg, well beaten

Preheat oven to 325 degrees.

Combine the oats, sugar, flour, salt and baking powder in a medium-sized bowl and mix well. In a small bowl or measuring cup, blend together the melted butter, vanilla and beaten egg. Add the butter/egg mixture into the dry ingredients, mixing well.

Cover cookie sheets with foil and prepare the foil with either butter or cooking spray. Scoop heaping teaspoons of dough onto the foil about 3 inches apart. These will spread! Bake for 15 minutes or until golden around the edges. Cool the cookies on the cooking sheet and remove only after they have cooled.

⁓

Best Sugar Cookies

This basic sugar cookie recipe comes from the Putnam's Grandma Mary Lou, who is known in the family as the "world's best cookie maker." She developed this recipe from a cookbook she purchased in her home state of South Dakota more than 50 years ago. We call these cookies basic because they can be adapted into your favorite holiday cookie. Top with candy corn for Halloween, green sugar for Christmas or red sprinkles for Valentine's Day for an easy-to-make holiday treat.

Trixie Putnam
Matthew 2011
Kent who graduated 8th grade in 1978

Makes 5 dozen

1 cup unsalted butter, softened
2 cups sugar
1 cup vegetable oil
2 eggs, at room temperature
1 teaspoon vanilla
4 cups all-purpose flour
1 teaspoon baking soda
1 teaspoon cream of tartar
Dash of salt
Colored sugar crystals, sprinkles, or choice of candy for decoration

Preheat oven to 350 degrees.

Cream the butter in the bowl of your mixer. Add sugar and mix completely. Add the oil, eggs and vanilla; combine well. In a separate bowl, mix the flour, baking soda, cream of tartar and dash of salt. Slowly add the dry ingredients into the butter mixture. Let mixture chill in the refrigerator for at least an hour.

Take a teaspoonful of dough and roll it into a ball. Roll the ball in your favorite colored sugar, sprinkles or cinnamon/sugar mixture. Place balls 2 inches apart on the cookie sheet, and then flatten them with the bottom of a glass that has been dipped in sugar. Bake for approximately 8 minutes. Rest on the cookie sheet for 2 minutes. Transfer to rack, cool and store in an airtight container.

Fudge Nut Bars

If you are in the mood for a chocolate fudge fix, these bars are for you. The layer of creamy fudge is decadent between two layers of nutty, oat-filled crispy crust. Unlike traditional cookies, the flavor is better once cooled and we liked them even better the next day.

Karen Gregory
Kathleen 2012

Serves 12

Crust

2 ½ cups flour
1 teaspoon baking soda
1 teaspoon salt
1 cup butter
2 cups brown sugar, firmly packed
2 eggs
2 teaspoons vanilla
3 cups quick-cooking oats
1 cup chopped nuts (pecans or walnuts, optional)

Filling

12 ounces chocolate chips
6 ounces semi-sweet chocolate
1 can sweetened condensed milk
3 tablespoons unsalted butter
½ teaspoon salt
2 teaspoons vanilla

Preheat oven to 350 degrees. Prepare a 15½ x 10½-inch baking pan with butter or vegetable spray.

Sift together flour, soda and salt. In a mixer, cream together butter and sugar. Add eggs; beating well after each addition. Stir in vanilla. Add flour mixture to creamed mixture and blend. Add oatmeal, hand stirring to mix. Add nuts if desired.

Melt chocolate chips and chocolate in condensed milk over low heat. Blend in butter, salt and vanilla. Mix well.

Spread ⅔ of oatmeal mixture into greased pan. Cover with chocolate mixture. Drop spoonfuls of remaining oatmeal mixture on top of the chocolate filling, gently smoothing to flatten.

Bake for 25 minutes. Cool before cutting.

Tester's Comments: *The crust was a bit sticky to work with when spreading in the pan, so my daughter placed a sheet of plastic wrap over the crust and rolled it with a rolling pin to keep it from clinging excessively to her fingers.*
Emily Goldberg

Blueberry Crumb Bars

Imagine being in the warmth of summer, standing at a stall in the farmers market, drooling over the freshly picked blueberries. Imagine a crumbling dough that melts in your mouth as soon as it touches your tongue. Add these two together and, with a cold glass of milk, you get a little slice of heaven. Rated a number 10!

Trixie Putnam
Matthew 2011
Kent graduated 8th grade in 1978

Serves 16

Dough

1 cup sugar
1 teaspoon baking powder
3 cups all-purpose flour
¼ teaspoon salt (optional)
1 pinch ground cinnamon (optional)
1 cup butter, diced in ¼-inch cubes, chilled
1 egg

Berries

½ cup sugar
3 teaspoons cornstarch
4 cups blueberries

Preheat the oven to 375 degrees. Prepare a 9 x 13-inch pan with butter or vegetable spray.

For the dough, stir together sugar, baking powder and flour, in a medium bowl. Mix in salt and cinnamon, if desired. Add butter and, with your fingers, rub the flour and butter together to get a rough crumb. Mix in the egg to get a crumbly dough. Pat half of dough into the prepared pan.

For the berries, stir together the sugar and cornstarch. Gently mix in the blueberries. Sprinkle the blueberry mixture evenly over the crust. Crumble remaining dough over the berry layer.

Bake in preheated oven for 45 minutes, or until top is slightly brown. Cool completely before cutting into squares.

❧

Tester's Comments: *You can serve this dessert in small squares like a cookie or like we did, in a piece larger than a brownie, warm with ice cream on top.*

Patty Turnquist

Blonde Brownies

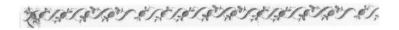

When Kelly Pettit was growing up, her best friend Sheryl's mother used to bake these brownies almost daily. She would cut them up and put them in the freezer, and, after school, everyone would go to Sheryl's house to raid the freezer for an after school snack of Blonde Brownies. Yummy!

Kelly Pettit
Angela 2008

Makes 15 pieces

2 cups flour
1 teaspoon baking powder
¼ teaspoon baking soda
1 teaspoon salt
1 cup chopped walnuts
²/₃ cup margarine, melted
2 cups firmly packed brown sugar
2 eggs, slightly beaten
2 teaspoons vanilla extract
1 cup chocolate chips

Preheat oven to 350 degrees. Prepare a 9 x 13-inch pan with butter or cooking spray.

Sift together flour, baking powder, baking soda and salt. Mix in walnuts. In another bowl combine melted margarine and brown sugar, let cool. Add eggs and vanilla. Add the flour mixture and mix thoroughly. Pour batter into prepared pan. Sprinkle chocolate chips over the top. Bake for 20 to 25 minutes. Cool in pan.

Tester's Comments: *Winners! I used unsalted butter for the margarine and Guittard chocolate chips. These were quick, easy and yummy. They're similar to a chocolate chip cookie bar, and if you cut them into small squares, they're like a soft chocolate chip cookie. They freeze beautifully for popping into a school lunch and are even good frozen. My kids raved about them and they are chocolate chip cookie aficionados!*

Susan Dennis

Caramel Corn

Linda Frasch received this recipe from an old family friend and has used it extensively. It's a great snack food and can make a good hostess or thank you gift in a decorative container. But be careful, it's addictive!

Linda Frasch
Lauren 2005
Eric 2007

Serves 12

6 cups popped popcorn
2 cups Cheerios
3 cups Rice Chex (or Corn Chex or combination)
1 cup cocktail peanuts (or pecans, almonds or mixed nuts)
1 cup butter (or ½ cup butter and ½ cup margarine)
1 cup brown sugar
¼ cup Lite Karo syrup
½ teaspoon salt
½ teaspoon vanilla
½ teaspoon baking soda

Preheat oven to 250 degrees.

Mix popcorn, Cheerios, Rice Chex and nuts together in large (heat proof) bowl, set aside.

In a deep pan, combine butter, brown sugar, Karo syrup and salt; boil for 5 minutes. Remove from heat and stir in vanilla and baking soda.

Pour sugar mixture over popcorn mixture. Mix to coat thoroughly. Spread in large roasting pan. Bake for 1 hour, stirring occasionally so that the bottom does not burn. Remove from oven and cool completely. Break apart and store in a tightly covered container.

Tester's Comments: *It's possible to eat this at any point in the assembling; it's delicious with or without the baking time. This is an addictive snack food and is great for watching TV or movies. The process and ingredients are similar to making toffee, and my husband, who is from Chicago, likened the taste to his favorite Garret's Caramel Corn in Chicago.*

Sharon Traeger

Priory Heritage Recipes

Five Decades
of Festivities and Feasts

The Woodside Priory School exists because of the dedication and generosity of many benefactors over the years. Indeed, in June 1957, before school even opened, Louise Davies hosted the first event for the benefit of the school, a fashion show featuring clothes from Elizabeth Arden. Guests were given a small program with a tiny gray pencil attached so they could make notes about the fashions, coiffures and make-up. Ladies up and down the Peninsula vied for tickets, and Mrs. Davies later presented Father Egon with a check for $4,000—a handsome sum in those days.

The first Spring Ball was held at the Los Altos Hills Country Club in 1962. Culminating in a candlelight champagne supper at midnight, the highlight of the evening was the auctioning of a purebred Aberdeen Angus steer. Complementing the Spring Ball that year was the first of twenty years of Christmas Bazaars. Mrs. Eyre and her Landscape Committee enlisted dozens of volunteers to make quilts, knitted items, Christmas ornaments and topiaries to sell to support their gardening activities. Two years later the Spring Ball became the Emerald Ball, which continues in spirit today as the annual auction.

Through contacts in Colombia, parents acquired a diamond-and-emerald-studded cross and ring. Each year these jewels were raffled at the Ball, and the winner of the raffle could keep them for a year "to wear, to display or to cherish."

The Woodside Priory Cookbook was first published in 1962 and featured recipes for elegant (and often time-consuming) dishes that were popular for formal entertaining. The second edition of the Cookbook appeared in 1978 under the energetic editorship of Judith DeSzily. The recipes from this edition reflect the new pressures on working mothers; many of the dishes in this edition include "oven to table" casseroles and more traditional foods prepared with new time-saving ingredients. Mrs. DeSzily recruited a cadre of helpers to assemble the cookbook under the Medieval-sounding moniker of "The Scriptorium Press." They laid out 260 neat stacks of pages on the tables of the dining hall and assembled four hundred copies of the cookbook by hand.

We have selected recipes from these first two editions of the Woodside Priory Cookbook for this edition, along with brief stories about some of the many contributors from the early years. We are grateful for their work on behalf of the Priory, and we join them in celebrating the culinary traditions of our individual families and of the entire Priory Community.

Coquille Saint-Jacques

The scallop shell has been replicated in art and architecture since the earliest times. Coincidentally, Mrs. Louise M. Davies, our own patron of the arts and architecture submitted the following recipe for scallops back in 1962. This recipe reflects the "Continental" style of cooking that was enjoyed in the 50's and 60's. Seafood such as the lobster, crab, shrimp or, as in this case, the scallop, was prepared in a creamy sauce, thickened with flour and/or egg yolk, sprinkled with Gruyere cheese and gratinéed in its own scallop shell or a ramekin until the top was bubbling and golden brown. It is interesting to note that in the jargon of Continental cuisine "Coquille Saint-Jacques" was commonly used to refer to this particular style of preparation. In France, however, coquille Saint-Jacques, or St. James shell, is solely the name used for this particular mollusk. The French nomenclature for this recipe would read: Coquille Saint-Jacques à la Parisienne because the creamy sauce is in fact sauce parisienne.

Mrs. Ralph K. Davies
Friend of the Priory

Serves 4 to 6 as a first course

1 pound sea scallops, preferably dry-packed
1 cup white wine
5 tablespoons of butter
1 cup minced onion
½ pound crimini mushrooms, thinly sliced
1 teaspoon salt
1 tablespoon flour
⅛ teaspoon cayenne pepper
½ cup scallop liquid or clam juice
1 egg yolk
Breadcrumbs
¾ cup grated Gruyere cheese

342

Wash scallops, reserving liquid, if any. Bring the wine to a simmer in a sauce pan and poach the scallops for 2 minutes. Remove scallops, let cool and slice into ¼-inch rounds. Reserve the wine.

Melt butter in a sauté pan over medium heat and sauté mushrooms, onions and salt until mushrooms are dry and onions translucent, about 10 minutes. Sprinkle the mushrooms with the flour and cayenne pepper; sauté for two more minutes. Add the wine in which the scallops were cooked and the scallop/clam juice; bring to a boil and stir until thickened. If too thick add a tablespoon or two of water or clam juice; if too thin, continue to reduce. Turn heat down to a slow simmer and whisk in egg yolk; cooking for two minutes to fully thicken the sauce

Preheat broiler.

At this point, the scallop may be placed in an elegant oval casserole, topped with the sauce, sprinkled with cheese and breadcrumbs and set aside until ready to broil. Or it can be portioned the same way into scallop shells or individual ramekins. Place casserole, scallop shells or ramekins on a cookie sheet and place into the broiler so the element is at least 6 inches from the dish. Broil until hot, brown and bubbling, about 5 minutes. Serve at once.

Clam Chowder

Mrs. Gerald Bates was the editor of the first Priory cookbook published in 1962. It contained recipes from a group of local women who called themselves "Friends of the Priory" and from some of the famous San Francisco restaurants such as Ernie's, Omar Khayyam's and Villa Taverna. Sadly, these restaurants have long ago closed their doors. This classic clam chowder, however, is a fitting representative of San Francisco's heritage. Recall taking out-of-town visitors to Fisherman's Warf or Pier 39 to enjoy clam chowder served in a sourdough bread bowl! It can be a great treat on a cold and foggy day.

Mrs. Gerald Bates
Friend of the Priory

Serves 4

½ pound bacon, diced in ¼-inch cubes
3 onions, chopped
6 medium cooking potatoes, peeled and cubed
2 (8-ounce) bottles clam juice
Water
3 (6-ounce) cans minced clams (see notes below if using fresh ones)
1 quart milk
½ cup cream
Salt and pepper
Oyster crackers

Fry bacon until crisp. Remove bacon, leaving the fat. Add chopped onion and sauté until the onions are tender but not brown, about 8 minutes. Drain the excess fat. Transfer to soup kettle with potatoes, clam juice and enough water to just cover. Bring to a boil then simmer until the potatoes are tender.

Add clams and their juice, milk and cream. Do not boil, but simmer for 5 to 10 minutes to develop the flavors. Add bacon bits and salt and pepper to taste.

Serve with a handful of oyster crackers.

꒱

Testers Comments: *If using fresh clams, use 2 to 3 dozen of the tender Littleneck clams. Wash thoroughly. Place in a large pot with 1 cup of white wine and bring to a rapid boil. Cover, reduce heat and simmer just until the shells open. Strain the broth through a cheesecloth and reserve the juice. Remove the clams from their shells and chop in preparation for the soup. The reserved clam liquid is then used when cooking the potatoes.*

Serve with plenty of crusty French bread (and butter) and a well chilled bottle of a semi-dry, fruity white wine such as California Sauvignon Blanc or French Sancerre.

Margaret Herzen

Hungarian Cherry Soup
with Cream & Wine
(Hideg Meggy-es cseresznyeleves)

In Hungary the appearance of cherries in the markets heralds the coming of summer, and cherry soup is a great favorite of the season. This traditional but unusual soup is almost like a cocktail and appetizer together, since the addition of wine at the end is not cooked off. It has an enticing aroma and is a perfect start for an elegant summer meal. In Hungary, it would have been followed by a spicy paprikás.

Mrs. Joseph Kovacs
Friend of the Priory

Serves 6

2 pounds sour cherries, pitted
1 cup sugar (or more to taste)
1 stick cinnamon
3 cups water
2 tablespoons flour
1 cup heavy cream
1 cup good quality red wine
Mint sprigs (optional garnish)
Lemon zest (optional garnish)

Simmer the cherries, sugar, and cinnamon in water until cherries are tender. Remove the cinnamon.

Blend the flour with 5 tablespoons of cold water until smooth with no lumps. If lumps exist in mixture, put the mixture through a sieve. Slowly pour flour mixture into the hot soup, stirring constantly. Bring mixture to a boil. Cook for 3 to 5 minutes stirring occasionally. Chill for several hours.

Before serving, stir in the cream and the wine. Place chilled soup in shallow soup bowls and garnish with a sprig of mint or sliver of lemon zest.

346

Hungarian Cherry Soup
(Sweet Cherry Version)

Because it is virtually impossible to find sour cherries similar to the ones used in Hungary, we have altered the recipe to impart more tartness to California sweet cherries. Do not over-sugar the cherries; there should be a good balance between the sweet and sour taste, with the final emphasis on sour. Puréeing the cherries is a more contemporary technique for thickening the soup eliminating the use of the flour resulting in a fresher finish on the palate.

Margaret Herzen
Elena 2003
Juliana 2007

---

3 pounds red cherries, pitted
Juice of 3 lemons
¼ to ½ cups of sugar
1 cinnamon stick
3 cups water
Salt to taste
½ cup heavy cream
1 cup of good quality red wine
Mint sprigs (optional garnish)
Lemon zest (optional garnish)

Macerate the cherries in the lemon juice for one hour at room temperature in a non-reactive sauce pan. Add two cup of water, cinnamon stick, and sugar. Bring to a boil, then simmer for 15 to 20 minutes until tender. Skim off the scum as it appears on the surface of the liquid. Discard the cinnamon stick.

Remove 18 cherries with a slotted spoon to use as garnish. Place remaining cherries into a blender and purée until smooth. Put all the puréed liquid through a sieve to remove unprocessed cherry particles.

Return the cherry purée to the soup. Chill for several hours. Follow serving directions in original recipe. In addition garnish with reserved cherries.

"Never-Fail" Popovers

Suzanne Eyre's resolute spirit strove for success in almost anything she undertook, whether it be the organization of the Gardening Committee at the Priory or culinary interests at home. In one, and in the other, with unerring taste, she would invariably find a path to success, as evidenced here in her "never-fail popovers."

Suzanne Eyre
Friend of the Priory

Serves 10

1 cup of flour
½ teaspoon salt
1 cup of milk
3 eggs

Preheat the oven to 350 degrees. Prepare a cast iron popover pan or muffin tin by placing it in the oven to heat.

Sift flour and salt in a bowl. Mix in the milk with a whisk. Add one egg at a time, mixing with a whisk until incorporated before adding the next. Take popover pan out of oven and prepare with cooking spray and a bit of meat fat, if you have it. Pour batter into prepared pan until each section is ⅔ full. Bake for 45 minutes keeping the oven door shut until the popovers are puffed and golden. Serve immediately.

Wilted Spinach Salad

It seems that some sort of a salad revolution had occurred among many of us in the early seventies. We dispensed with the ever present iceberg lettuce and turned our curiosity and newly developed tastes toward such leafy greens as the lovely Bibb lettuce, the loose-leaf, the Romaine, the escarole and, of course, spinach. This salad that Mrs. Barbagelata submitted was all the rage in the seventies and is still wonderful.

Mrs. Robert Barbagelata
Robert 1980

Serves 8

1½ bunches spinach, cleaned, de-stemmed and torn into bite-sized pieces
6 green onions, minced
1 tablespoon of garlic oil
6 raw mushrooms, sliced
4 strips bacon, chopped
1 tablespoon extra-virgin olive oil
1 tablespoon tarragon vinegar
1 teaspoon red wine vinegar
1½ teaspoons sugar
2 tablespoons Grand Marnier
1 hard cooked egg, grated for garnish

Coat mushrooms in garlic oil.

Saute bacon until crisp. Remove from skillet with slotted spoon and reserve. Reheat the bacon drippings and add the vinegars, sugar and Grand Marnier; reduce for two minutes over medium heat. Pour over the salad adding bacon bits and mushrooms on top.

Serve immediately in a large salad bowl or divide among individual salad plates. Top with grated egg

Lasagna Speciale

Mrs. Annamaria Q. Kusber, a poet and a painter, is a vivacious woman who enjoys telling of her cooking experiences. Creating her own recipes was her specialty and this is her version of a lasagna dish she submitted for the 1978 cookbook. She lives in Woodside with her husband who grows orchids. She is the mother of two Priory alums.

Mrs. Annamaria Q. Kusber
Angelo 1980
Paul 1985

Serves 10

Ingredients for Pasta

1 pound flour
1 teaspoon salt
3 eggs, beaten
2 tablespoon of olive oil
2 to 3 additional spoons of water

Sift flour and salt into a large mixing bowl. Make a well in the center and pour in beaten eggs and 2 tablespoons olive oil; mix flour and liquids together with your fingertips until the pasta dough is just soft enough to form into a ball, adding a tablespoon or two of water if the mixture seems too dry.

Sprinkle a large pastry board with flour and knead the dough on the board with the flat of your hand until dough is smooth and elastic (about 15 minutes), sifting a little flour on your hand and board from time to time. Divide dough into 4 parts and, using rolling pin, roll out one piece at a time into paper-thin sheets. To do this, roll out in one direction, stretching the pasta dough as you go, and then rollout in the opposite direction. Sprinkle with flour; fold over and repeat. The dough should be just dry enough not to stick to the rolling pin. Repeat this process of rolling, stretching and folding the dough another 2 or 3 times and until dough feels smooth and glossy. To make lasagna noodles, roll out the dough to a paper thin sheet and cut into 4-inch by 10-inch strips. Place on a clean cloth to dry for at least 1 hour before cooking.

To make the dough in the food processor, add the flour and salt in the bowl of the processor and mix. In a measuring cup with a pour spout, mix the eggs, olive oil and 2 tablespoons of water. Turn the machine on and, through the feed tube, add the egg mixture slowly and process for one minute. Add the additional water if pasta does not come together when pinched. Using a pasta machine follow the instructions for making lasagna noodles.

Cook the pasta sheets in boiling water just until al dente, about 2 to 3 minutes. Transfer to ice water to cool. Dry before using.

Filling

1 small onion
6 tablespoons butter, divided
¼ cup dried crimini mushrooms, steeped in boiling water for 30 minutes
1½ pounds cubed raw chicken, a mixture of light and dark meat
½ cup Madeira wine
1½ to 2 cups chicken broth
¾ pounds fresh chicken livers
4 cups of béchamel sauce (white sauce)
Salt and white pepper
Butter for assembly
1 cup grated Parmesan cheese

In a sauté pan over medium heat, fry onions in 2 tablespoon butter until golden brown, about 12 minutes. Add mushrooms and cook for 5 minutes. Add chicken and 2 more tablespoons butter; sauté over medium heat until

(continued)

beginning to brown. Deglaze the pan with Madeira and cook until evaporated. Pour in 1 ½ cups chicken broth and cook until reduced by one quarter, about 4 minutes. Simmer, covered for 25 minutes, or until the chicken is tender and most of the broth has evaporated. If necessary add more broth one tablespoon at a time during the simmering process. Let cool.

In a separate skillet fry chicken livers in 2 tablespoons of butter until firm, but still medium rare on the inside. Combine with the cooked chicken mixture. Add 4 cups of your premade béchamel sauce. Combine gently. Season to taste with salt and white pepper.

Assembly

Butter bottom and sides of an 8 x 10-inch pyrex casserole. Lay one layer of lasagna noodles in the pan and spread a with a layer of the stuffing; dot with additional butter and sprinkle with Parmesan cheese. Continue alternating the layers until you end with a lasagna layer. Brush the top with melted butter and let stand for 6 hours.

Preheat oven to 400 degrees. Bake lasagna covered, for 30 minutes, until bubbling and hot. Let rest for 5 minutes before cutting.

Chicken Saltimbocca

Mrs. Adam Heidenreich's contribution of recipes for the 1978 edition of the *All New Woodside Priory Cookbook* is very impressive, indeed. Every chapter features carefully written and precisely described preparations of dishes from appetizers, main courses and desserts. The following is one of the classic Italian preparations of chicken. Enjoy!

Mrs. Adam Heidenreich
Friend of the Priory

Serves 4

4 boneless, skinless chicken breast halves
4 paper-thin slices of prosciutto or good smoked ham
¼ teaspoon powdered sage
Salt and pepper to taste
¼ cup unsalted butter
½ cup dry white wine or dry vermouth
2 tablespoons additional butter, cold

Pound chicken pieces between sheets of waxed paper or plastic wrap. Place prosciutto on each and roll up to make a neat package. If chicken is pounded well, it will stick to itself (no skewers needed) but if not, use a toothpick to keep in place. Season with sage, salt and pepper.

Preheat oven to 350 degrees.

Melt butter in a medium-sized ovenproof sauté pan over medium-high heat until foaming and sauté chicken until golden all around, about a minute or two per side. Pour vermouth into pan and place into the preheated oven for an additional 10 minutes to finish the cooking. Transfer chicken to heated serving platter and reduce the pan juice in the sauté pan to a glaze. Turn off the heat, whisk in the butter and pour over the chicken. Serve immediately.

Chicken in Sour Cream

Margaret Kiely, and her late husband, John R. Kiely, were indefatigable supporters of the Priory from the onset. The couple had many hobbies and interests. One such hobby involved traveling with their family and fishing. In 1991 Mrs. Margaret Kiely wrote and published a book called *Coattails*, a novel about fly-fishing in various interesting parts of the world. Here is a sampling of the recipe she included in our prior cookbooks.

Mrs. Margaret Kiely
Michael 1962

Serves 6

4 chicken breasts, bone in
4 chicken thighs, bone in
½ cup of butter or ¼ cup of butter and ¼ cup of grape seed oil
¼ teaspoon ground rosemary
¼ teaspoon ground thyme
Salt and pepper
2 tablespoons chopped parsley
¼ cup slivered almonds
1 tablespoon chopped green pepper
½ cup dry sherry
½ cup chicken stock
1 cup sour cream
½ cup grated Gruyére cheese (optional)

Heat butter and oil in a skillet over medium-high and brown chicken on both sides, about 10 minutes. Remove from skillet and place in a casserole. Deglaze the pan with the sherry over medium-high heat and reduce by half, scraping up the brown bits as you go. Add the chicken stock and reduce again for 3 minutes. Remove from heat and cool. Season browned chicken with rosemary, thyme, salt and pepper. Sprinkle the parsley, almonds and green peppers over the chicken. Slowly mix the sour cream into the cooled sherry and stock reduction. Pour over the chicken in the casserole. Cover and bake for 30 minutes. Sprinkle with grated cheese and broil, if desired, until the top is a golden brown.

Serve with a mushroom risotto.

Beef Bourguignon

Mrs. Coralia Kuchins and her late husband, Harry, are among the original founders of the Priory. They had two sons: the late Harry, Class of 1965, and Andrew, Class of 1977. In the Spring of 1999 Andy, while employed at Stanford University as Associate Director of the Center for International Security and Cooperation, followed in his parents footsteps and coordinated the Alumni Fund. Unfortunately for the Priory, a position as Director of the Moscow Carnegie Center took him away from his old high school stomping ground. What does Andy say about his mom's cooking? "Mom did not like to cook very much, but her Beef Bourguignon was great." Here is her recipe for you to enjoy.

Coralia Kuchins
Harry 1965
Andrew 1977

Serves 8

2 to 4 tablespoon olive oil or butter
3 pounds beef from shoulder, cubed
3 ounces lean bacon, diced
1 yellow onion, finely chopped
1 tablespoon flour
2 cups good quality red wine
1 cup beef stock (frozen Perfect Additions)
2 garlic cloves, crushed
Bouquet garni (tie together sprigs of fresh thyme, 1 2-inch leek, fresh
   parsley and 2 bay leaves)
Salt and pepper
½ pound of small white onions (frozen okay)
2 tablespoon of butter
½ pound mushrooms, sliced
Parsley, chopped for garnish

Heat 2 tablespoons olive oil in a large casserole over medium-high heat. In two batches, brown the cubed beef on each side until brown. Remove beef and add bacon and onion with additional oil or butter if needed. Sprinkle with flour and sauté until onion is lightly browned and bacon is cooked, about 10 minutes. Add meat and any accumulated juice, wine, beef stock, crushed garlic and the bouquet garni; bring to a boil. Season with salt and pepper, reduce heat, cover and cook over low heat for 1½ to 2 hours or until the meat is very tender. Remove the meat and reduce the sauce to about half, or until thickened to taste.

Parboil small white onions for 3 minutes and drain. Heat the 2 tablespoons of butter in a small sauté pan, add onions and caramelize over medium heat for 10 minutes. Add mushrooms and sauté together for a few minutes leaving the mushrooms still firm.

Skim off any fat from the reduced sauce in the casserole pan. Combine the meat with the reduced sauce in the casserole. Add the onions and the mushrooms and simmer for an additional 15 minutes, covered. Garnish with parsley.

Testers Comments: Serve with peeled, boiled and lightly parsleyed small red or white potatoes, steamed green beans and a luscious full-bodied Côte du Rhone, Bordeaux—St.Emilion or Beaujolais. This is an excellent dish to prepare a day or two ahead of your dinner party since the flavors are enhanced with time. It is also a lovely dish to serve for a buffet in a chafing dish.

Margaret Herzen

Traditional Hungarian Gulyas

Gulyas (or goulash) is a soup, and the more it is reheated, the better it will taste. Its origin can be traced back to the ninth century, when Hungarian shepherds cut their meat into cubes, cooked it with onion in a heavy iron kettle (bogracs) and slowly stewed the dish until all the liquid evaporated. They dried the remnants in the sun, and then put the dried food in a bag. Whenever they wanted food, they took out a piece of the dried meat, added some water and reheated it. With a lot of liquid, it became a gulyas soup. If less liquid was added, it became gulyas meat.

Mrs. Thomas DeSzily
Anthony 1978

Serves 8

2 tablespoons lard, bacon fat or olive oil
2½ pounds beef chuck roast, cut in ⅔-inch cubes
3 medium onions, peeled and chopped
1 garlic clove
Pinch caraway seeds
Salt to taste
2 tablespoons sweet paprika
2½ quarts of water or good quality, low-sodium beef stock
1 medium, ripe tomato, peeled, seeded and chopped
2 green peppers, cored and sliced into rings
1 pound Yukon Gold potatoes peeled and cut into ¼-inch dice.
Tabasco to taste

Melt lard, bacon fat or olive oil in 6- to 8-quart Dutch oven. Add beef, in two batches, and brown well on each side, about 10 minutes per batch.

Remove beef and sauté onions until glossy, but not browned, about 5 minutes.

Add beef and accumulated juices back into pot.

In a mortar and pestle, crush the garlic with the caraway seeds and a little salt.

Remove the pot from the heat. Stir in the paprika and the garlic mixture. Stir rapidly with a wooden spoon. Immediately after the paprika is absorbed, add 2 ½ quarts of warm water or beef stock (cold water toughens the meat). Bring to a boil then lower heat and braise on low heat for about 1 hour, covered.

At this point add the tomato, green peppers and more water or stock to give a soup consistency. Add a little salt to taste.

Simmer slowly for another 30 minutes. Add potatoes and cook the gulyas until the meat is very tender and potatoes done.

Adjust salt. Add Tabasco to taste.

Serve with galuska, noodles or rice.

Veal Paprikás

Mr. and Mrs. Lazlo started the nation-wide chain called the Magic Pan, which specialized in making a variety of crepes. Palacsinta, as crepes are called in Hungarian, are almost a national dish. It would not be surprising to learn that, given the quantity of palacsintas that his restaurants would fry, Mr. Lazlo invented a crepe cooking wheel that cooks crepes on a revolving stove. Currently, they operate Babbo's and Bravo Fono at Stanford Shopping Center. The Fono-Lazlo family were also owners of the popular Paprikás Fono restaurant in Ghirardelli Square. This delicious Hungarian stew was prepared there.

Mrs. Paulette Fono
Friend of the Priory

Serves 8

5 tablespoons grape seed oil
3 pounds veal leg, cut into 2-inch cubes
3 medium onions, finely chopped
3 tablespoons Hungarian paprika
1 whole green pepper, cut in half with seeds removed
1½ cups water or chicken stock, plus 1 tablespoon
Salt to taste, at least 1 teaspoon
½ teaspoon white pepper
1 rounded tablespoon flour
½ cup sour cream

In a 4- to 5-quart heavy casserole or Dutch oven, heat oil over medium-high heat, add half of the veal and brown evenly on all side, about 5 to 7 minutes. Remove to a bowl and continue with the remaining meat and remove. Sauté onions in for oil for 5 minutes over low heat, stirring frequently, until golden; add paprika and continue cooking for 1 more minute. Add the green pepper halves, 1½ cups of water or chicken stock, salt and white pepper. Cook at a low simmer, uncovered, about 40 minutes. Taste for seasoning and remove the green pepper, discarding it. Taste veal for tenderness, it should be tender but not falling apart.

Mix flour and sour cream with the remaining 1 tablespoon cold water or chicken broth in a separate bowl. Add 2 tablespoons of hot paprika sauce from the cooked meat to the sour cream and mix well. This will prevent the sour cream from curdling in the sauce pot. Add sour cream mixture to veal and cook, stirring constantly, until warm and thick.

Serve veal paprikás at once or reheat over low heat before serving. If veal paprikás is not served the day it is cooked, do not add sour cream until the day it is served.

The paprikás can be served with galuska, also called spätzle (drop noodles), pasta noodles or rice.

Venison Stew

For the hunters out there, Mrs. Gerald Bates, the editor of the 1st Edition of the WPS Cookbook, offers venison stew as a variation on the theme of the Beef Bourguignon. As with the beef, select shoulder meat to be cut up for the stew. Prior to preparing this dish, marinate the 3 pounds of venison for at least 24 hours in the red wine marinade.

Mrs. Gerald Bates
Friend of the Priory

Serves 8

3 pounds venison, cut in 1½-inch cubes
1 carrot, sliced
2 onions, sliced
1 stalk celery, sliced
½ cup olive oil, divided
1 bottle red wine
½ cup red wine vinegar
Bouquet garni
12 juniper berries
12 whole peppercorns

In a saucepan, sauté the carrot, onion and celery slices in half the oil until soft, but not browned.

Add the wine, vinegar, bouquet garni, juniper berries and peppercorns and bring to a boil. Simmer until the vegetables are tender, 15 to 20 minutes. Add the remaining oil and leave to cool thoroughly.

Place the cubed meat in a deep bowl and pour the marinade over so that the meat is covered completely. Refrigerate for 24 hours.

When ready to cook the venison, remove the meat and vegetables from the marinade, discarding the vegetables. Drain the venison and pat dry with paper towels. Then proceed with the recipe for Beef Bourguignon (page 356). Strain the marinade and measure 1 cup, discarding the remaining. Add fresh wine to measure 2 cups total. Stewing time may need to be increased to up to 3 hours.

A note on venison: If you do not have hunters in your family, look for farmed venison which is becoming more readily available and popular because it is lower in cholesterol than traditional beef.

Autumn Apple Pie

The late Barbara Oswald's experience with fine food and dining goes back to the days when her father operated one of the finest restaurants in San Francisco, The Blue Fox, located in the Financial District. After she married Ralph Oswald, the two of them owned a series of restaurants, the most favorite with Peninsula patrons being the Skywood Lodge and the Village Pub (sold just recently in 1999) in Woodside. The Oswald's support of the Priory began in the early sixties when their two boys, William, Class of '78, and Christopher, Class of 79, began their education at the Priory. They are one of the early founders of the Parent's Association and subsequently acted as co-presidents. They brought their culinary experience to the Priory and hosted many fundraiser and/or appreciation dinners and barbecues either on the Priory grounds or in their own home. On such occasions Ralph would take charge of the main course, while Barbara enjoyed preparing the salads and the desserts. Here are two of her signature pies that we hope will continue to delight all those who prepare them in her memory.

Mrs. Ralph Oswald
William 1978
Christopher 1979

Serves 8

1½ cups water
1½ cups sugar
2 bay leaves, divided
1 sliced lemon
1 tablespoon apricot preserves
Pinch ground cloves
8 tart and crispy apples, peeled, cored and sliced
Pastry for one double crust 9-inch pie
3 tablespoons softened butter

3 tablespoons brown sugar
Pinch nutmeg
1 egg yolk

Preheat oven to 400 degrees.

Bring the water and sugar to a boil; add 1 large bay leaf, lemon, apricot preserves, cloves and nutmeg. Let this boil gently for 20 minutes, then strain. Poach the apples in this syrup for 12 minutes, covered. Drain well and cool.

Place apples in a pie shell. Dot with the softened butter and sprinkle on the brown sugar and nutmeg. Place the bay leaf in the center of the pie. Cover with pastry top and crimp the edges together in a decorative manner. Brush the crust with the beaten egg yolk and cut air vents.

Bake in preheated oven for 10 minutes, then lower to heat to 325 degrees and bake for an additional 25 minutes. Let cool and remove bay leaf if possible.

Lovely in the Fall. When serving this pie contemplate the charming apple orchard that neighbors the Priory to the north of our tree-lined driveway.

Bretonne Blueberry Pie

Tastes have changed over the years and for a more contemporary dessert, try reducing the sugar to ½ cup and adding one tablespoon of lemon juice with the Cointreau.

Mrs. Ralph Oswald
William 1978
Christopher 1979

Serves 8

4 cups blueberries, divided
¾ cup sugar
½ cup water
2 tablespoons cornstarch dissolved in 2 tablespoons cold water
1 tablespoon Cointreau
¼ cups slivered almonds, toasted in a 350-degree oven for 8 minutes
1 9-inch baked pie shell

Crème Chantilly (recipe follows)

Mix 1 cup berries with sugar and water. Bring fruit slowly to a boil and cook until berries are soft, about 10 minutes. Rub the mixture through a sieve or purée in a blender and then strain. Add cornstarch liquid and cook purée until thick. Stir in butter and Cointreau. Cool. Add almonds then gently, but thoroughly, combine the uncooked berries. Pour the mixture into the baked pie shell and chill the pie for several hours.

Before serving, cover with Crème Chantilly.

Crème Chantilly

1 cup of heavy cream
2 tablespoons of sugar
¼ teaspoon of almond extract

Whip cream until very soft peaks are formed, adding sugar and almond extract as you beat. Do not over beat the cream. It should form very soft and light peaks

*"You ought to have seen what I saw on my way
to the village, through Mortenson's pasture to-day:
Blueberries as big as the end of your thumb,
Real sky-blue, and heavy, and ready to drum
In the cavernous pail of the first one to come!
And all ripe together, not some of them green
And some of them ripe! You ought to have seen!"*

Robert Frost

Marzipan Torte

In the 1978 edition of the Woodside Priory Cookbook, on the opposing page of Judith DeSzily's Walnut Torte, is Barbara Oswald's famous Marzipan Torte. Judith recalls enjoying it frequently in the Oswald's restaurant, "Skywood Chateau," and also recalls that it was her son's favorite cake.

Mrs. Ralph Oswald
William 1978
Christopher 1979

Serves 10

1 ⅓ cups flour
1 teaspoon baking powder
½ cup unsalted butter
⅓ cup sugar
1 egg
½ cup raspberry jam

Marzipan Filling

½ cup butter
⅔ cup sugar
½ teaspoon almond extract
1 cup almond paste (softened)
2 eggs
3/4 cup sliced almond, toasted in a 350-degree oven for 7 minutes
1 cup cream, beaten to soft peaks with 2 tablespoons of sugar.

Preheat oven to 350 degrees. Prepare a 9-inch springform pan with butter and flour or cooking spray.

In a medium-sized bowl, mix the flour and baking powder. In the bowl of a mixer, add butter and sugar; mix until smooth, about 3 minutes. Add egg and mix until well incorporated. Add dry ingredients in two batches until just incorporated. Do not over mix. Press dough evenly in pan. Spread ¼ cup of jam over dough. Cover with saran wrap and chill while making the filling.

In the bowl of a mixer, cream butter and sugar until light and fluffy. Add almond extract and paste; mix until completely smooth. Add eggs, one at a time, beating well after each addition. Spoon almond filling over jam layer in the springform pan, carefully.

Bake in the preheated oven for 50 minutes. Cool, then spread the remaining ¼ cup of jam over the top.

Sprinkle toasted sliced almonds over the top and serve with a dollop of whipped cream.

My Uncle's Favorite Walnut Torte

A collection of recipes with a connection to a Central European past would be remiss not to include Judith DeSzily's walnut torte. This cake is characteristic of the many Hungarian varieties of nut-based desserts.

Mrs. Thomas DeSzily
Anthony 1978

Serves 10

6 tablespoons powdered sugar
6 egg yolks
2 cups ground walnuts
6 egg whites, beaten stiff, but not dry

Frosting

¾ cup scalded milk
2 cups ground walnuts
¾ cup powdered sugar
1 stick unsalted butter, cut into pieces
1 teaspoon rum or vanilla

Preheat oven to 350 degrees. Prepare a 9-inch springform pan with butter and flour

Beat together the powdered sugar and yolks in a mixer until the yolks are light and the volume has doubled, about 5 minutes. Gently fold in the walnuts. Whip the egg whites until stiff, but not dry. Take ⅓ of the egg whites and mix vigorously into the thick batter to lighten it up. Gently fold

370

in the remaining beaten egg whites. Fold just until the white is no longer evident, trying to keep the volume of the cake batter high and light.

Pour the batter into the prepared cake pan. Bake in preheated oven for about an hour or until cake springs back when touched (or a wooden toothpick comes out clean). Cool for 10 minutes, then unmold and cool on a rack. Fill and/or frost with the cream frosting.

For the frosting, pour scalded milk over ground walnuts. Cool until completely cold. Place walnut mixture into the bowl of a mixer and add ¾ cup powdered sugar, butter and vanilla or rum. Beat until the cream is completely white and light, up to 30 minutes. Fill and frost cake.

Keep the cake in the refrigerator until about 15 minutes before serving.

Champagne Punch

Stories are told that on many social occasions in the early days of the Priory, a special Champagne Punch was served that quickly became a tradition. Here is the one that appeared in the '62 Edition of the Woodside Priory Cookbook that is particularly delectable and refreshing.

Make 20 4-ounce servings

½ pint peach brandy, chilled
1 fifth Sauterne, chilled
1 fifth Champagne, chilled
1 (1 quart bottle) lemon lime or ginger ale soda
Ice block or ring
2 ripe peaches, peeled and sliced

Pour the brandy and Sauterne into a large punch bowl. Slowly add the Champagne and then the soda. To keep cool add an ice block or ring, cubes will melt and dilute the flavors. Garnish with peach slices in the cups or in the punch bowl.

374

Index

Index